The World.
Around it.
On a Ship.
Mostly.

(Copyright© 2017 James Wearne)

The World. Around it. On a ship. Mostly.

To Coral

Her desire to see the world and learn about everything in it has rubbed off on me.

The World. Around it. On a ship. Mostly.

Introduction

My name is Jim. At the time of writing, I'm 65 years old, for some odd reason. Certainly it's not by choice. I'm in good health – otherwise I couldn't have gone on the trip, more of that to come. I'm large, just large enough to have been, for the past fifty years or so, occasionally called "Big Guy." If you know any men who are large enough to be called that, do them a favor and don't. We hate it.

I'm an American from Chicago, college educated at a State School and that means basically what you assume it means. I've never been to war, and the first time I saw a mountain or an ocean I was over 21. I used to be married, and I have two daughters who are extraordinary human beings. I also have two grandchildren who, though both are under two years old, have already, between them, written six symphonies, solved cold fusion and have been accepted into The Sorbonne and into Heidelberg University, having mastered the necessary languages, plus Latin and Greek. They are also approached daily by agents begging them to model for fashion magazines.

This is a journal of my trip around the world on a freighter. A container ship, to be more precise. The ship departed from Newark NJ, headed mostly east, and wound up, 65 days later, in Seattle. What qualifications do I have to write about freighter travel? Only that I have done it and, since you're reading this, you probably haven't. I had read numerous articles and books about freighter travel before booking this trip, and they were all helpful and excellent. They were also mostly written by nice, polite people who, I now realize, now that I've also traveled by freighter, left out a lot. Not that they tell you only the good stuff, but they just don't want to hurt anybody's feelings or put anybody off the idea of travel by freighter. I figure that, if you read this and you decide

The World. Around it. On a ship. Mostly.

(before the trip) that freighter travel isn't for you, I will have done you a big favor. You're welcome.

I'm writing this book from both ends. As I start this introduction, I'm still on the ship, about 8 days out of my final destination port, from which I fly home. I'm also, of course, still writing the day-by-day entries. After I get home, I will go through the whole thing and flesh out the day-by-day stuff, making entries like "Laundry. Dryer." Into full sentences which may make sense. I will also probably add general reflections and such, both having to do with the trip and other things.

As the title implies, this is a 'Round the World trip. I boarded ship in New Jersey - Newark, in fact, and will have, in about 8 days' time (make note of that word "about." It speaks volumes) docked in Seattle, thence to fly home, (Notice the "thence?" College.) having crossed the Atlantic Ocean, the Indian Ocean, the Strait of Melacca, the South China Sea, the East China Sea, the Sea of Japan and the Pacific Ocean. That's a lot of water under the bridge. (Get it? – the ship has a Bridge and the water went…. Oh, never mind.)

Around the world. In fact, more miles will be sailed (and a few flown) than it would take to go straight around the equator. If I can figure out how to make the map program I've got tell me, I'll tell you at some point how many miles it was. It was 26,000 miles. I considered taking the train for the USA legs, so that it could be around the world entirely on the surface, but I have, multiple times, in a car and on a train, travelled from Chicago to both coasts and back on the surface. So I will have covered the entire mileage on the surface.

There are things I'm not going to tell you. One of them is the name of the cruise company with which I made the arrangements. Many are reasons I shouldn't. Such as: I didn't get on with them, they were not particularly cordial or helpful to someone sending them a lot of money, there were many things that they could and should have told me but didn't, and they provided some information, as we will see, that was simply incorrect. I will certainly suggest that if, at the beginning of your dealings with a cruise company or booking agent for your journey, you get a bad taste in your mouth about the people with whom you're dealing, change companies. Do this before you send them money, of course. I didn't follow that advice, and the whole process of booking and making pre-arrangements was unpleasant and more stressful than it ought to have been. As this is a public document, and not a private, confidential letter, I could be potentially open to legal trouble if I were to mention that company's name. My aim, readers, is silence.

Another thing I won't mention is the name of the freighter company. Yet another is the name of the ship. This is for a different sort of reason. The personnel of the ship on which I was a passenger were, without exception, helpful, friendly, respectful and altogether pleasant and professional. In this journal I will mention things that are not necessarily positive. I do not intend that these things should reflect badly on the officers or crew of the ship, nor on the company which owns and operates the ship. The great majority of the criticisms I may have are part and parcel of freighter travel, and not due to any lack or incompetency on the part of anyone involved with the ship or of its owners.

Any personal names I use in writing this are altered. I may make reference to crew members, to members of my family or to other people by name. Be assured that the names I use are not the actual names of those people. For the benefit of any of those people who read this, please don't spend any time wondering things like "Why did he change my name to Ethel? Does he think I look like an Ethel?" All of the name changes were purely arbitrary.

I have tried to represent the trip and my reactions to aspects of it honestly. When there was a disappointment (and there were disappointments), I didn't thrash about and curse in my cabin and then write "I was a bit disappointed."

I have also omitted such details as the fact that about a quarter of the way on I developed a rash on various parts of my body – I think from the detergent with which they wash the sheets – and I do not give you a square-inch-by-square-inch account of its appearance, its location and its advance and retreat. It was there about three weeks. It's gone now. Thanks for asking. It itched very badly, and I had no anti-itch cream along nor any way to get any. Take along anti-itch cream.

Pursuant to that last thought, here's a fact. If you do not bring something with you that you might need, you may have to go without it for the duration of the trip. The number of things you can buy on board is very limited, and you must not count on port stops as opportunities to purchase necessities. I lost my pocket comb somewhere on board about halfway through the trip. I am without one as I write, and will remain without one until I get to Seattle.

Make a list of the things you need to pack. It should include things that you use not only every day, but even only occasionally. Of course you will list your prescriptions and daily supplements as well as obvious things like toothpaste, but also list things like heartburn remedies, anti-diarrheal pills and laxatives. Hopefully these aren't things you use often, but if you use them at least once a month, say, list them, buy them and take them along. I'll list here some of the things that I took.

AAA and AA batteries	Binoculars
Anti-diarrhea meds	Books
Bathroom scissors	Bug repellant

The World. Around it. On a ship. Mostly.

- Camera with battery and charger
- Deck shoes
- Dramamine
- First-aid kit
- GPS and data cable
- Heartburn remedy - chewables and pills
- Info on destinations
- iPod, cord and charger
- Kindle, cord and charger
- Laptop, power cord, mouse
- Laundry bag
- List of email addresses
- Mini recorder
- Money for misc. expenses
- Money for tips - $5.00 per day, cash
- Nail clippers
- Needle and thread
- Noise-cancelling headset
- Normal toiletries
- Pain reliever
- Paper map
- Paperwork
- Plug adaptor
- Prescriptions
- Shampoo
- Sleeping pills
- Small amounts of each local currency for anticipated port stops
- Soap
- Spare glasses
- Sunblock
- Sunglasses
- Swim trunks
- Thumb drive
- Vitamins
- Washing powder packets

Some of them I didn't use, but I was glad I had them. I have omitted a couple of items just because, well, just because. If you wonder – "Why didn't he take X?" – Well, I probably did, but it's none of your business.

As far as some of the items – you may wonder, for example, why I took washing powder packets. "If they provide washers and dryers, surely they must provide the washing powder to use in them," you say. Well, they did. But nowhere in any bit of information that I saw while preparing for the trip did it say that they would. Therefore I took the easy precaution of packing and taking along a plastic bag with enough packets of washing powder to do laundry once a week. Nor did it mention anywhere whether the machines were free or coin-operated. They were free, but I couldn't know that. These are the things that you have to anticipate and think through. Take nothing for granted. That's worth repeating. Take nothing for granted.

The cruise company I used to make the booking instructed me that I was not to ask them questions such as would there be washing powder. They said that the ship company, with whom I was not to get in touch until 10 days before sailing, would provide me with that sort of information. The ship company subsequently informed me that they did not respond to passenger inquiries of this sort, which should be answered by the cruise company.

The cruise company seemed to feel that any answer to any possible question on my part was in their on-line brochures and that if I would just get off my lazy butt and read them all of my questions would be answered. They weren't. Many of the questions I had could not be answered by reading the brochure, and a very important piece of information (really – it was HUGE) that was in their brochure was incorrect. I tried to find alternate on-line sources of information and was partially successful but, from my experience, there are precious few people out there who know about this stuff and will tell you about it. Except for me. You're welcome.

If you want to buy something on board, there's what is called, on some ships anyway, the "Slop Chest". It is generally not a shop, or even a room that you can visit. It's a list, with item names and prices, which can be gotten from one of the ship's officers. You

The World. Around it. On a ship. Mostly.

ask him for the items, he will get them to you and will make note of the cost, and will dun you when you leave the ship.

Here's the list of Slop Chest items from the ship I was on. I have left off the prices, as they will have changed, but they were Wal-Mart level.

Slop Chest Merchandise List

Cigarettes

Marlboro Red/Gold

L&M Blue and Red

Davidoff

Wine

Red Wine Tisdale

White Wine Tisdale

Wine Bordeaux Superior 75 CL

White Wine HK

Soft Drinks and Mineral Water

Coca-Cola, 7-Up, Fanta, Sprite, Pepsi, Lipton

Sparkling Water 1X1.5 ltr

Mineral Water Still 24X05 ltr

Snacks and Chocolates

Planter's Cocktail Peanuts

Pistachio Pack/Can 130gm

Peanuts w/Shell 500 gm

Popcorn

Dortios

Pringles

Mixed Nuts Planters

Chocolate Kit-Kat HK

Snickers / KitKat / Hersey's / Twix / Mars

Kinder Chocolate

Chocolate Cadbury HK

Chocolate Toblerone

Chocolate Riter Sport

Skittles

Chocolate Milka

Chewing Gum Winterfresh / Orbit

The World. Around it. On a ship. Mostly.

Miscellaneous

Roll-on Deodorant 50ml

Old Spice / Mitchum Stick 95gm

Shower Gel

Shower Gel Palmolive 750ml

Tooth Paste Crest

After Shave Nivea, Gillette, Brute

Shaving foam Gillette

Razors Gillette Blue

Shampoo / Conditioner: H&S / Pantene

Nivea Body Lotion 330 ml

Dove Shower Gel New

Nivea / Old Spice – Deo Spray

Colgate Toothpaste 180g

Toothpaste Signal

Toothpaste Sensodine

Oral B Toothpaste 100GM

Tooth Brush

Listerine 500ml

You may look at this and wonder exactly what some of the entries mean. I have no answers to that sort of question. I just copied everything down as it appeared on the list I was given. Also note the limited number of beverages containing alcohol. Other writers of freighter travel books and articles may refer to buying beer or spirits from the Slop Chest. Do NOT count on it.

The fact that I have given you this list is more significant than you may realize. When preparing for my trip, I Googled every combination of words I could think of meaning "What can I buy on board as a passenger on a freighter?" and came up empty every time. It's like it's a big secret. Try it, and maybe you'll have better luck than I. But that may only be because I have published the above list on my personal web site and you found that.

The World. Around it. On a ship. Mostly.

You may notice that on the list were cigarettes. The officers on my ship were almost all from the same Central European country. I won't mention which one, but it's a former Soviet State. They, like many Europeans, all smoked. A lot. If you have an aversion to second-hand smoke, or can't stand a dirty ashtray, you will have some bad moments.

I suspect that this is not unique to this ship, as, according to sources I have read and talk I have heard, most ships of this sort have, no matter the country of registration, as officers, Europeans from one or another former Soviet State. Usually on a given ship, they are all from the same country. Also, and more about this later, these sorts of ships have crews made up almost entirely of Philippinos. That is, of course, not a problem, just a fact.

In the list of things I brought, I included a seasickness remedy. If you are prone to seasickness, I have a feeling that you will not enjoy the trip as much as you ought. Cruise ships and liners such as you may have been on, even perhaps on rough seas, have stabilizers. Freighters don't have stabilizers. Having said that, the bigger the ship the better. Also newer. New, big ships are designed to minimize the effect of rough seas. Not for your benefit, but for the sake of the cargo.

Still, as we shall see, even someone like me, who has never been seasick, even when being bounced around like a cork in a tiny fishing boat in Mount's Bay, Cornwall, could feel the effects of the sea. More about that later. Nothing disgusting.

Also, many newer ships of the passenger variety use "Pods" attached to the hull for propulsion, and don't have the one massive propeller at the stern, powered by a diesel engine as big as a house. One effect of those pods is an almost complete lack of vibration in the ship.

Freighters have the propeller and the diesel engine, and every second of the trip you will feel a variety of vibrations as a result. You will come to be used to it, and even learn to recognize different varieties of vibration which indicate speed, change of direction and complete lack of forward motion. You will learn to hate that last one.

I mentioned somewhere above a map program. I'll talk about it here, along with another bit or two of technology I'm using. First of all, I have a large paper map on the wall. It's held up by clips that stick to the wall magnetically. The walls are steel. Now for the tech.

I bought, some months ago a hand-held, battery powered GPS device. It's called a Garmin GPSmap 78sc. It will take a GPS reading anywhere in the world. On its screen it will give you a map display of your position (small and not too detailed) and will also show you many other things like heading, elevation, etc. It will do many things for you and is intended mostly for people who are fishing, sailing, trekking and other such. You can buy detailed maps of areas and regions to install into it. Garmin also supplies, free to download into your computer (you will be taking along a laptop,) a program called Base Camp, which will coordinate with the hand held device (USB cable required) and allow you to show your position on its more detailed map.

There are many more things that Base Camp and the handheld can do than I am using, but what I am doing is establishing daily waypoints (little flags) with the handheld and transferring them to the Base Camp map on my laptop in order to mark our progress. I do this every morning at about 6:00 am. It's good to do it at the same time every day to give an accurate idea of daily progress. It is also helpful in showing exact Longitude and Latitude and distances. It also helps to show where to make a mark on the paper map each day. Why do both? Well – I have the map on the wall, and I have the Garmin.

A passenger who was on the ship with me for the first few stops showed me an app for smartphones, which I downloaded before getting out of reach of phone coverage. It's called AndroiTS GPS Test. It, too, reads GPS signals and tells you many things like speed and heading. It will also, when in cell phone coverage range, show your position on something like Google Maps. I can't use that feature out here in the middle of the ocean, but I saw it working and it's cool. I believe that there are purchased versions of the app which do more.

But how did all of this get started? With Michael Palin. Formerly of Monty Python's Flying Circus. He has, in more recent years, done a series of excellent television travel programs, one of which was based on Verne's "Around the World in 80 Days." One leg of Mr. Palin's trip was to cross the Atlantic on a freighter. I actually remember very little about that part of the show. I do remember thinking that I'd like to do that. Over the next few years, I would occasionally Google "freighter travel" and wonder how I would like it. I eventually came to the conclusion that I would like it just fine.

I have traveled on passenger ships, including an Atlantic crossing on the Queen Mary 2. I enjoyed it, but there was much involved with it that I just didn't need. I never gambled in the casino nor paid extra to eat in the 5-star restaurant. I never went to the musical productions, the night club or the Spa. I'm sure all of those things are just fine, but not my style. Even the formal nights in the Dining Room were a bit much. Freighter travel is well known for its complete lack of anything vaguely resembling any of those things and it's much cheaper as a result.

I planned to retire in October of 2016, when I turned 66. I figured that it would be a good idea to celebrate my retirement and put a sort of line in the sand between my working life and retirement by taking a trip around the world on a freighter. This was reinforced by a letter from a former employer reminding me that I had a 401(k) plan with them. The amount in it almost exactly matched what I believed that the trip would cost. I emailed the booking company that shall remain nameless (and hereafter referred to as "The Agent") and started the process of arranging to sail in February of 2017 (date based on various considerations.) Well – the company I was working for suffered a downturn and laid off a bunch of us in February 2016. I changed the trip date to June of 2016.

The process was not supposed to be lengthy or difficult. I made lists and began to acquire various objects which I thought might be useful – the Garmin, for example. I received information from the agent about what I needed to do, and when.

My first clue as to the potential nature of my relationship with the agent was some ambiguities in the specifics of that information. For example, a medical form was needed, to be filled out by my doctor stating that my general health was good enough so that I was unlikely to have any sort of attack or to drop dead while on the ship. These ships generally don't have doctors or hospital facilities, and you're sometimes thousands of miles from land, so you need to be healthy.

The wording in the information I received from the agent included something about that form and a date of 60 days prior to the trip. In another place it said 30 days. It was also not clear if the form needed to be received, filled in, PRIOR TO 60 (or 30) days before sailing or WITHIN 60 (or 30) days before sailing. An important thing to get cleared up, you'll agree. My initial question regarding this was met with a response that was basically: "That answer is in the information we provided. Please read the information and you will find your answer. Idiot. Plus you're ugly and you smell bad."

The World. Around it. On a ship. Mostly.

I may be overstating, but that was the tone. The information was not in the brochure, nor in any documents I had thus far received. After a few more emails, I finally got the true dope, which was that the form had to be submitted within 60 days of sailing. I should point out that, in order to mollify the staff at the agent in order to obtain an answer to my questions, my general demeanor can be described as extended and repeated groveling. I don't grovel well, and it was stressful.

Another bit of confusion was in regard to whether I would need a Visa if I wanted to go ashore in Viet Nam. The agent didn't know. They didn't quite know how to go about finding out. They had booked many people on this trip before – why didn't they know? Research entirely on my part finally arrived at the answer that I would not need a Visa. I told the agent. They didn't thank me.

There is a third and largest (really – it's MAJOR) bit of, in this case, misinformation from the agent which will come up later. It's a big one. Stay tuned.

(Oh, yeah – and – I read in a couple of books and articles about how, when initially going to the ship and boarding, someone picked up the author/passenger at their hotel and drove them directly to the ship, whereupon their luggage was whisked aboard by crew members and maybe a cargo net.

Nobody picked me up. A taxi, the driver of which had never been inside the Newark Container Port, drove me there and we spent a number of minutes and dollars trying to find the proper gate, whence (college) the port security van drove me to the ship, where I schlepped my own bags up the precarious, bouncing, rounded-stepped, greasy boarding ladder. Me, at 65, making two trips up that rickety, swaying, dirty contraption, carrying large, heavy suitcases. Cargo net, my ass.)

Over the next few pre-trip months, I filled in forms, visited the Visa bureau for China in Chicago (you need a visa for China, but not for Hong Kong) sent money to the agent, got a Yellow Fever shot, sent money to the agent and generally got ready and sent money to the agent. I had to think about pre-paying some bills and otherwise arranging to be away from home for over 2 months. That's a lot to think of.

When the time finally came, I did some last-minute double-checking, did some soul-searching such as: What am I, crazy? Do I really want to leave my home and family (including an adored toddler grandson and newborn granddaughter) and go off on some ship?

But I went. From here on, it's my log as I wrote it – pretty much – with, as I said, some reflections and explanations intermixed. Actually the format is as it is because I'm too lazy to do footnotes. I'll also put in the emails I sent home. I hope you find it interesting and informative, especially if you are considering freighter travel.

The World. Around it. On a ship. Mostly.

Trip Log 6/12/2016 – 8/20/2016

Day 1 - 6/12/2016 Sunday, Starting at home.

Got up at 2 AM. Groan. Took a shower. Most of the packing was already done. I finished what remained; toothbrush and such. I was on the road by 3 AM. Arrived at O'Hare long-term parking at 3:30. I messaged the family with the car's location, grabbed my 3 bags and headed for the people-mover.

> [Sometimes, when going on a longer trip, especially if it involves a really awkward departure time, I will drive to O'Hare and park in the long-term (cheap) parking. I will have left my keys with someone, making sure I have my spare to use to get the car to the airport, then, once parked, call or message them with the car's location. They will then, in the next couple of days, at their convenience, go to O'Hare, pick up the car, and take it home. I will subsequently pay them back for the parking fee.]

The line at the front counter was medium-bad, but since I had to check a bag, it was unavoidable. I used the self-serve kiosk, successfully for a change. Usually those don't read my ID and therefore don't work for me at all. I noticed that there were two lines for people with bags to check. One was moving faster. I used that one, and it went pretty quickly.

When I got to security, they seemed to be having a "fire sale." Bags on conveyer. Phone and key into pocket of carry-on. No shoes off, belt off, anything. Straight through and out. I walked miles and miles to gate G17 for the Newark flight and got there about 4:30 am. Some people were there already. I wonder what time they had gotten up? Nothing like a coffee stand or any such was open yet. Groups of employees were, at intervals, coming in through a door marked for the BA shuttle bus. It looked like busloads of workers arriving from the parking lot. I wondered if I'd see Eddy.

[A son-in-law. He was working the early shift at O'Hare at the time.]

The World. Around it. On a ship. Mostly.

Waited. And waited. Gate agents started showing up and using the computer. They were just clocking in. The real gate agents for our flight didn't show up until about 10 minutes before boarding. Got a boarding pass OK in the exit row.

> [Getting a boarding pass for the flight I want isn't always a given. Because one of my daughters works for the airline, I fly nearly free, but it's always standby. Hence the early flight. If I hadn't made that one, there were several more that day, one of which would probably have had a seat.]

I said hello to Eddy as he came through the door on his way to work, just before boarding. The man in charge of the gate seemed a bit panicked. We boarded. I had to valet my rolling carry-on as it was a small plane. I had seat 13a – the window. However, 13b had in it a very big guy who lapped over about 25% of my seat. It was a generally uncomfortable flight, but at least it had good legroom because of being on the exit row. Also it is only about a 1 ½ hour flight to Newark, so it was bearable. Even though it was a sunny day, there was a lot of turbulence coming down through the clouds. Approaching the airport, there was much bumping and fighting of winds. On deplaning, a passenger said that he had heard the Pilot say that it was "The worst in 10 years."

As we waited on the Jet Bridge for our valeted bags, the pilot walked by, with a look on his face as if he expected to be congratulated. Actually, I, or someone, should have. Sorry, Captain.

I got my bags and took the "Air Train" shuttle to the hotel shuttle pickup point. The container terminal from which I'd sail is very close to Newark airport, and I took a picture of the cranes in the port from the Air Train at the airport. Got the shuttle to the hotel. Tipped 5 bucks because of my heavy bag. The hotel seemed OK. Very slow elevator. The room also seemed OK. I mention this because the ratings on the Web had not been good. I could see the cranes at the container port from my window. I ate lunch at the

The World. Around it. On a ship. Mostly.

hotel restaurant. There were no other choices nearby. Bad cheeseburger. Back to the room, showered, napped. Nothing further worth reporting happened.

The World. Around it. On a ship. Mostly.

Day 2 - 6/13/2016 Monday, at the hotel in Newark

Up at 8 AM. Breakfast in the hotel coffee shop – scrambled eggs and corned beef hash. Called the ship company and got info regarding boarding, as it was not absolutely stated in advance exactly when the ship left. When I asked if there were any other passengers, the man said "I didn't know there was you until you called." We would sail at 2:00 PM on the 15th, according to the best info at that point. I got the hotel stay extended one night and got a late checkout for Wednesday. I called Vera, about going with her and a friend to the World Trade Center site.

> [Vera is a Facebook friend, whom I'd never met in person. Very nice and helpful. It was good to have a friendly contact in the New York area.]

I got a cab to Vera's place, which ran $55.00 plus tip. Met with her and her friend and we took a nice walk thru Jersey City to the subway station. We took PATH to the WTC site. We decided to go up to the observation deck of One World Trade Center. In the elevator, the inside walls are actually video screens, showing a simulated outside view. At first, the view is of the island before any people lived there, then it changes as time goes by through New York's history. By the time you're at the top, the view is as if you are looking out of windows.

We walked around the observation deck and took pictures. The weather was clear and sunny, so it was possible to see a goodly distance in all directions. Up there, you are high enough to see over any nearby buildings, but not so high as the area around the tower is hidden. I saw several old favorite places from up there, and had a very pleasant couple of hours. After we came down we walked to the Mysterious Bookshop. I took pictures of my book on the shelves.

> [I wrote a mystery novel called The Adventure of the Old Campaigners and it is on the shelves at the Mysterious

Bookshop in New York, a very prestigious location. It's also available on line. It's a good book. Makes a wonderful gift.]

We had lunch at trendy place in SoHo, the name of which I've forgotten. I had carrot soup for lunch. That's how trendy it was. No cheeseburgers available.

We walked to the pools where the original WTC buildings stood. If you haven't been, in a pleasant park area are two square pools, very large and deep. These follow the outside dimensions and plan of the locations of the two Towers which were attacked on 9/11/01. Inside there is water (at times) cascading down the sides and into a smaller square receptacle at the bottom of the pool. It's very stark, and not at all pretty. Around the sides are metal panels with the names of all who died there represented as cut-outs in the metal. A very good metaphor for their absence, I thought. Among the names displayed around the sides of the pools, we found Rick Rescorla's name and paused to reflect and to honor him.

[Rick Rescorla was one of the great heroes of 911. His foresight and heroism saved thousands of lives, at the cost of his own. Look him up on line. You will be moved. We looked for him especially because the two ladies I was with are both from Cornwall and my principal ancestry and name are Cornish. Mr. Rescorla was a Cornishman, and is a hero to the Cornish and to Cornish-Americans.]

I said goodbye to ladies and took PATH to Newark Penn station, then took a cab to the hotel. A long day, but a good one.

The World. Around it. On a ship. Mostly.

Day 3 - 6/14/2016 Tuesday

Up at 8 AM. Had the same breakfast at the hotel restaurant (very small, usually with one waiter-manager and one cook) but had the eggs poached. Called the ship company. I talked to another man, who sounded much smarter and seemed to know what he was talking about, who said "Board tomorrow after 10AM. So I decided to go back into New York City for the rest of the day. I booked a shuttle into Manhattan. We went through the Lincoln tunnel, just by way of orientation. The shuttle dropped us next to the Port Authority Bus Terminal, at 39th and 9th at about noon.

I walked to the Nero Wolfe neighborhood on w. 35th St. and saw the plaque that the "Wolf Pack" had put up. There's a house across the street, a brownstone, with 7 steps (Plus one that looks like it was added at some point when they fixed the sidewalk.) Not quite right, it's on the wrong side of the street, but it's close enough to the description in the books to be suggestive.

> [One of my favorite authors is Rex Stout. He wrote a series of mystery novels and stories about a detective named Nero Wolfe, who weighed around 300 pounds and seldom left his house/office on W. 35th St. His legman Archie Goodwin did the moving about, and Wolfe did the thinking. They are wonderful stories and it would be worth your while to read them. The first one is called "Fer de Lance." Start with it.]

I walked toward Greenwich Village. At one point, as much to make a point to myself as anything, I stopped and bought slice of New York style pizza, and folded it in the paper plate to eat. I got grease on my shirt. It was very hot, but I managed to eat it while walking. It's harder than it looks. But, in the future, when debating Chicago style vs New York style pizza, I can honestly say I have had the experience, and enjoyed it, of eating a folded-up slice on the streets of New York.

On the way, I stopped in a couple parks to rest. It was another very pleasant day, and the leafy greenness of the parks was thoroughly

The World. Around it. On a ship. Mostly.

enjoyable. Some had tables set up for office workers to bring their lunch to, and all seemed to have some sort of activity going on. In one, they were playing live Jazz. I decided to stroll down as far as Greenwich Village, for old times' sake.

> [The first night I ever spent in New York City, decades ago, was spent on a doorstep on Spring St. Why I did that is another story. The fact that I completely forgot to see if I could find that doorstep again on this trip still confounds me.]

When I made it to Washington Square, I people-watched. There are still folkies playing on the benches in Washington Square, also buskers. A cool thing happened. A hip-looking black lady about my own age was sitting on a bench, and as I walked by, our eyes met, and she saluted me. I smiled and bowed a little. Did she recognize another former hippie? A fellow member of our rapidly-diminishing tribe? Had I been in the Square in the 60s, we might have passed a joint and sung together.

I saw the Bitter End. A lot of great music got played there, and maybe still does. It looks like it's still open. Walked bit farther, to Broadway and Houston, then turned back uptown. I zigzagged through many blocks again, and again stopped at a couple of parks to rest. Found a Mexican place near the pickup point and had roast chicken for supper. I still had an hour or so to kill, so I walked some more, went into a Starbucks and got an Americano and sat by the window.

An Asian girl with a camera walked by. Then she casually walked back and then walked by again, with her phone in front of her. Very sly. She took my picture, I saw it on her screen. It wasn't the first time I have had my picture taken probably mistaken for a colorful "local" (I'm fairly colorful-looking, compared to the norm.) One other time was in Roskoff, Brittany, where a young tourist snuck a picture of me sitting on a bench. He probably told people, when he showed his slides back in Akron, that I was a typical Breton peasant. How disillusioned both he and the New York girl would be to find out I'm from Chicago.

I walked back to the shuttle pickup point by the Bus Terminal with about a half-hour left to wait. I was feeling footsore, and wanted to sit down, but no benches or any such were to be seen. I walked up the block and found chair just randomly sitting in a small vacant patch. I moved it to the pickup point and sat in it and waited.

After the shuttle came and I got in it, as we waited for other passengers, a man came along sat in the chair. A young, suit-wearing business guy. He put on a pair of socks. Over the socks he was already wearing. Actually, I was glad to have been able to create that bit of surrealist theatre right there on the streets of New York.

Back at the hotel, I checked the ship's arrival time, which they estimated as the next day at 3:30 AM.

Day 4 – 6/15/2016 Wednesday

N40° 40.903' W74° 08.813'

I got up at 6 AM, tried to go back to sleep, and got out of bed at 7. Same breakfast. Went back to room to pack. Checked internet and email for last time in the hotel. Internet access and email would be limited to nonexistent once en-route. Not being sure of the status of meals on board while in port, I bought candy bars and energy bars just in case.

Surprisingly (or not) I felt very nervous. I checked out of the hotel and ordered a cab. The cab came, and it turned out that the cab driver had never gone to the container port before. His GPS got us inside and he asked directions to the gate. It was a bit difficult to find, and was merely a small guard shack amid the vast and massive terminal area. He let me out at the gate. The guard had my name on his list, fortunately, and asked to see my passport to confirm my identity. I stood outside in the sun amid this giant, dusty, busy, noisy industrial area until a security van came and got me and took me to the ship, racing around sky-high stacks of containers and dodging trucks carrying containers.

Down the side of the ship was hung a set of stairs, very difficult to climb. The stairs themselves were not flat, but rounded, I suppose so that they would be equally usable (if equally awkward) if the staircase were at a different angle. I waited at the bottom while some local stevedores came down. I carried my smaller case and shoulder bag up and discovered in the process that the stairs were also very bouncy, and very dirty. I left the smaller cases at the top and went back down and carried the big case up. Once I had schlepped all of my luggage up, a man at top said he was going to help me. I wondered why he waited until that moment to mention it.

At that point, the ship felt very much like a construction site. Hard hats, coveralls, reflective vests. At the top of stairs a man at a table checked my name against his list. Fortunately, I was on it. The area – still outside, on the deck – was a very small, awkward, busy space. Once on the ship, it felt like being in a large factory. Very dirty (in places), very busy.

I was shown into a small office where a young man checked and took my passport and other papers. All in order, much to my relief. The steward – "Mark"? (Turned out to be "Marco") – took me up in the elevator to my cabin on deck F. Pleasantly, it was as advertised. Clean, spacious, new, well-appointed. He told me lunch would be at noon (it was about 11 by this time.) I showered and changed. The water pressure and heat of the water in the shower was luxurious. I looked around a bit in the "Accommodation" which is what they call the white structure which houses the crew quarters and offices and has, at the top, the bridge. I had thought that it would be called "The Castle," but I was wrong. I found the laundry room.

Back in my room, I discovered that the desk chair was missing a foot. (No wheels on any chairs on the ship. They would roll around in rough seas.) Marco got me a new one immediately. I asked about a key for the room, and they made a new one. Apparently a previous occupant had carried off the only key. At noon, I went to lunch in the Officer's Mess on deck B.

This was also as advertised. Not plush, but clean, new, well-appointed and an effort had been made to make it look more or less like the dining room of a nice B&B or some such. There were white tablecloths and real flatware and glassware. There was nobody else there. Time in port is very busy, and then especially the officers and crew eat when they can. In a stainless-steel tureen on a sideboard was chicken meatball soup. The main course was tempura-style shrimp. Tasty. I went back upstairs via the stairs

The World. Around it. On a ship. Mostly.

and explored a bit more. Found the bridge. There was nobody there and I wasn't sure if I was allowed, but a crewman came in and didn't seem to mind that I was there.

I checked out passengers' recreation room, a few doors down the hall from my cabin. It was small, with little in it. There was a cabinet with books, but all of the books except one ("Trinity" by Leon Uris) were in French. I don't speak French. I saw swimming pool. It is inside, a sort of a cubical tank, currently empty.

I asked a young man when we sailed and he said tomorrow, 2100 hours (9:00PM) I first took him for French, but he, like most of the other officers, turned out to be from a former (and to be, here, nameless) former Soviet State.

My room had a mini-fridge, although it never seemed to get very cold. At one point, the Captain pointed out that it wasn't a "refrigerator," it was a "cooling unit." I never found out any more than that. My electric adaptor seems to work, thankfully. Two large bottles of water were in the room. It turned out that a constant supply of bottled water would be provided, free. The water generated by the ships desalinization plant was potable, but not pleasant.

I went up to bridge again. Nobody there. Back in my room, I took a nap till 5. I started reading the books I brought along, although I wondered if I was starting a bit early. The first was an excellent book on Tintagel in Cornwall by Charles Thomas.

Went to supper at 6. Same soup. It would always be the same soup at both lunch and supper. A stew of some sort. Tasty. Bread – French Baguette – very good. Cheese after. Only instant coffee, but I've had worse. I was initially confused as to whether dinner started at 6:00 or 6:30. I went at 6 and it seemed all ready. Again, nobody else was there. Marco tends to hover a bit while serving meals, but it will probably be different when others are there.

The World. Around it. On a ship. Mostly.

After supper I explored some more and found the "library." It was mostly a storeroom, with a few industrial books on shipping. Back in my room, I figured out how to open the windows. It involves four heavy-duty catches that screw and unscrew. Before bed, I watched some "Dr. Who" – I may watch them in order.

> [Years ago, I videotaped many Dr. Who episodes off the air as they were broadcast by Channel 11 in Chicago. They were recorded onto VHS, but recently I transferred them to video on the computer and brought them along on the laptop I took on the trip. It became a nightly ritual to watch a part of an episode before bed.]

All of this time, loading and unloading of containers was going on. Trucks bring the containers to the dock beside the ship, and massive cranes grip the containers in a way that almost seems tender and gentle, by their upper corners and swing them, very speedily above the ship and straight down, sometimes into the very bowels of the ship, making tall stacks that rise above deck level and right in front of my forward windows. I had two forward windows. I saw basically jack out of them except containers the whole time. I saw a lot out of the side window, however. Clever of me to arrange to have a side window (which was actually pure luck. I didn't arrange anything of the sort.)

So endeth the first day on the ship, still in port in Newark.

The World. Around it. On a ship. Mostly.

Day 5 – 6/16/2016 Thursday

N40° 40.903' W74° 08.813'

Still in Newark Container Port. Got up at 6 because breakfast is at 7. Had fried eggs and toast. Apparently there is also bacon available, but I didn't find out in time to order any. I met the other passenger, named Max. He was a nice guy, and he filled me in about a lot of things. He was to get off at Savannah.

I was alarmed to hear him say that on the eastward trip we don't go through Mediterranean and the Suez Canal as the brochure described, but around the south end of Africa. I made a note to ask "Ivan," the 3rd officer – the one who checked me in.

I saw where email is done – in same office on the "upper deck" where I checked in. There's one computer there on which the satellite email server can be accessed. Emails are strictly text-only – no attachments. Turns out I must get my email account ID and such from Ivan. While talking with Ivan, he hinted that no liquor is to be bought on board. It's a "Dry Ship." Hmmmmm. In a few minutes I will meet with Max and go to a mall somewhere in New Jersey. Maybe pick up something there and smuggle it on board?

Mall visit over, smuggling successful. We (Max and some crew members and I) went to a mall, which turned out to be a fashion outlet mall. Not my sort of thing. I walked a bit into the town of Elizabeth NJ and found a liquor store. So now I had contraband.

Turns out Max was right about the route. We wouldn't go through the Suez, but around the bottom of Africa. I'm told that it takes no more time. I wonder if I will bother complaining to the agent? It seems a rather grievous error on their part to have sent someone (me) off on a long and expensive trip based on wrong information.

> [This was the error that I said in the introduction was yet to come. I could have gotten extremely angry about it – in fact, I'm still plenty PO'd – but the other choice was to make the best of it

The World. Around it. On a ship. Mostly.

> and not let it spoil the trip. I chose the second option, but it wasn't easy. I had to convince myself that to storm off the ship at that point and start raising hell would probably cause me much more pain, grief and inconvenience than it would the agent. Did I mention that I wouldn't recommend the agent I used? I sure wish I dared name them.]

We were to sail at 11PM. It was going to be 9, but it got pushed back. It would be a struggle to stay awake. Supper – poached fish and rice. Brought a cup of coffee to the room to help me stay awake if possible.

I did stay awake. I hung around in my cabin till about 10:45, then looked out and saw a tugboat. Went up to the bridge. It was completely dark there, except for the glow of the radar and the other instruments. This is normal, I found out, for nighttime maneuvers and running.

I don't know exactly what time we left, I forgot my watch in my cabin. I tried to take pictures, but just got blurs. I should have studied the camera manual a bit more thoroughly. We backed out very slowly into the channel. I sang the "Farewell Shanty."

> [To hear me singing "Farewell Shanty" in a pub in Wallaroo, South Australia, go to:
>
> https://www.youtube.com/watch?v=9oVj3TNeUiE . Skip the ad.]

NYC glowed in the distance. Tugs guided us out of our berth into the channel, through something called "kill van kill" or something like that.

> ["Kill Van Kull" I was close.]

The tugs stayed with us until we were in New York Harbor. We went under a small bridge which was under construction. I saw neighborhoods asleep on both sides of river. We towered over the buildings on the banks. Oil tanks clogged the riverside. There was a strange thing going opposite us, near the bank. A sort of barge, stubby, rectangular (sort of like a 2/3 long shoebox), and fairly tall.

No lights, no obvious place for people to be, no windows, just a large rectangular object, but it seemed to be navigating. Very strange.

We moved slowly out into the Upper Bay. The Statue of Liberty glowed in the distance as I regretted again not having reviewed the "Night Shooting" section of the camera manual. We passed tugs and barges and turned right toward the Verrazano-Narrows Bridge.

There were striking reflections under the bridge from the lights on the roadway. After we passed under the Verrazano-Narrows Bridge, being sure to note how close the top antenna mast atop the ship's bridge came to the underside of the bridge, I came inside. The breeze was picking up, it was getting chilly, and there was nothing much more to see. I was outside whole time, about 1 ½ hours. Back in my cabin I celebrated our departure with some contraband whisky. There was some vibration from the engines, and some slight rocking.

The World. Around it. On a ship. Mostly.

Day 6 (1st day at sea)- 6/17/16 Friday

N39° 47.608' W73° 51.346'

I woke up just before the alarm at 6. Slept well. Smooth sailing. For breakfast I had eggs and remembered about the bacon. Max showed me around the office on the Upper Deck and around the Bridge. I arranged with Marco (the Steward) for a coffeemaker, which I had noticed in a cabinet in the Passenger Recreation Room. It was a standard drip machine, with a British-style plug. That's good, in that it would handle the ship's 220-volt current. Plus my plug adaptor was able to manage it.

I used my GPS unit to get our position and marked the position on BaseCamp's map.

> [This would become a morning ritual. Each day at about 6:00 am I would take a GPS position reading and mark it on the map in the Garmin BaseCamp software on my laptop. As a result, I now have a complete map of the journey framed on my wall, showing the position marker (a little flag) for every day of the trip.]

Marco brought me a whole case of bottled water. This would become routine, that I would at all times have ample quantities of bottled water in my cabin. For one thing, it made better coffee than the ship's water.

Raphael, the Safety Officer, gave me a safety orientation tour. They provide each passenger with a hard hat, a coverall (called a "Boiler"), shoes and gloves. There's also an "Immersion Suit" in case we had to abandon ship. (Spoiler alert! We didn't!) We toured safety locations, and even went into the lifeboat. After, I took a safety test in the office – during which he fed me the answers.

I went to the bow and the stern with Max. There wasn't much room to walk along the outside edges of the cargo deck, but you can get all the way around. They just ask that you A: Wear your

The World. Around it. On a ship. Mostly.

hard hat and B: let them know you're going and that you're back. At the bow it was very peaceful and quiet. No engine noise, and it's somewhat sheltered from the wind. Quite pleasant. And no, I didn't do the "Titanic" thing. Max couldn't lift me.

Roast duck for supper. Very posh.

The Coffee maker worked! Marco had brought in some ground coffee for me to try in it. I also tried turning on the fridge in the rec room and put water in the ice tray. I may have mentioned that the fridge in my room wouldn't make ice. Fingers crossed!

We spent some time "drifting" off Norfolk. Apparently we missed our berth and had to wait for another one. No way of knowing when we would get in. I sent my first email to the folks back home, a "testing – testing" sort of thing. Not sure if everybody got it or just Alice who was the first address in the list. I used commas as separators, maybe I'll try semicolons next time.

The World. Around it. On a ship. Mostly.

Day 7 (2) – 6/18/2016 Saturday

> [I will notate the days as above, the first number being the number of days since leaving home and the second number (in parentheses) being the number of days at sea. The difference will always be 5.]

N37° 24.253' W74° 53.687'

I made coffee in my room this morning! Breakfast, eggs and sausage. The sausage was basically a hot dog. Back to bacon tomorrow.

> [And every day after that. My daily breakfast, almost unaltered for the whole trip, was one fried egg, one piece of bacon, one piece of toast, made by me in the toaster in the Officers' Mess, and juice. I probably won't mention breakfast often after this.]

The fridge in the passenger recreation room made ice! I had despaired of having anything cold to drink (or ice for whisky) but it looked like it would be OK.

Still "drifting" off Norfolk. The likely thing was that we would get there late that night. Didn't know if we would be able to get into town. While drifting, in order to maintain position, the engines had to fight against currents, making a lot of bumps like a train starting and stopping. Annoying but no big deal. I considered doing laundry.

Went up to the bridge. Nothing to see but sunny 365° horizon. The sunglasses worked great! The ones I brought would fit on over regular glasses (and didn't look like those huge tinted goggles that were popular some years ago among old people.) As a consequence, they sealed out wind much better than regular sunglasses. The bridge was often windy, and to have that wind kept out of my eyes was wonderful. It turned out that the bumps were just waves hitting the side. They didn't seem that big, but some have a lot of energy it seems. The info board on the Bridge just said "Norfolk 6/19."

The World. Around it. On a ship. Mostly.

It turned out that the coffee grounds provided were decaf. That explains why the coffee the previous night hadn't kept me up! The only caffeinated coffee on board was instant. So I resolved to, at the earliest opportunity, buy some regular ground coffee.

Ivan said we would get to Norfolk late and only stay a few hours but we would be in Savannah for 24 hours. I figured I wouldn't go ashore in Norfolk, but should be able to shop in Savannah. Or Charleston if time would permit.

It turns out that the pop in rec room fridge is for me. Cool.

A little after 1:00 PM, I put my laundry into the washing machine machine. It was a front loader, with European instructions. I thought I might have overloaded it, but decided to wait and see.

Slowly we closed in on Norfolk. Hopefully to be there or near before dark, for pictures.

5:30 PM. The laundry took a long time – hadn't got the hang of the machines. Everything got clean and dry, though. Still going slowly toward Norfolk. Land on the horizon – Virginia Beach?

Things were getting golden as we slowly moved into Norfolk harbor that evening. There was a large, flat bay into which several rivers flowed, and I could see evidence of various maritime activities on the distant shores. We rounded a point and angled into a channel that took us past some of the Navy yards and upstream into the container port as the sun set. We went past small Navy ships and submarines docked in the yards. Our officers cautioned us not to take pictures of them. Apparently the Navy watches people like us from shore and has been known to send a boat to a ship like ours to confiscate cameras. The container port is up the bay some. It was dark by the time we got to our berth. I watched them steer the ship to the dock and tie off. It's more interesting than it seems. 10:00 PM. Now to get some of that ice………

The World. Around it. On a ship. Mostly.

Day 8 (3) 6/19/2016 Sunday

N36° 52.392' W76° 20.912'

Woke in the container port in Norfolk. Loading and unloading were going on full speed, with the associated slammings and boomings. Our officers said that we could go ashore as long as we were back by 2 PM. I caught the port shuttle which took us to the gate of the port and thence got a cab with the chief engineer and his helper and Max. We went, of course, to Walmart. I bought a mattress pad, as the bed is very hard, magnet clips for my map, COFFEE (two large cans,) a wine box, and miscellaneous other items. Suddenly I got a call from the ship saying that we had to be back sooner than anticipated – 1:00 PM. This was about Noon. I told Max, and arranged for an earlier pickup with the very nice cab lady (with a son in the Merchant Marine) who had brought us to the store. Ate McDonalds for lunch, then got another call from the ship telling me that we had to be back even earlier -12:30. I wasn't with Max at that point, and they said his phone didn't work. Ultimately we all got in touch and the cab came even earlier. We all back to the ship OK. Back on board by 12:30. But that will start to give an idea how things were likely to go as regards "Shore Leave." We passengers were subject to the same rules as the crew, and they would leave without us if necessary.

The mattress pad went on the bed, the map went up on the wall, my Cornish flag went up (also on the wall – covering the "Art" that was in the room – a picture of another of their ships.), the wine box went into the fridge, and coffee was at the ready. All well. Bring on the Atlantic!

I watched our departure from Norfolk (2:45 PM) past the outer causeway.

The World. Around it. On a ship. Mostly.

Supper started with "ox tripe soup." Main course - pasta (rigatoni?) with a mushroom cream sauce. Finished reading "Father Hunt."

> [Re: the soup. It seemed to me that someone on the ship – maybe the captain – must have LOVED tripe soup. It was on the menu far too often for my taste. I discovered that the broth was good, though.]

Day 9 (4) 6/20/2016 Monday

N33° 58.274' W76° 22.894'

At sea this morning, smooth sailing, clear sky. Rocking a bit more than yesterday. I went up to the bridge. The Captain said rocking is "Good for sleeping." Outside on the port side I saw flying fish near the bow, ahead of the bow wake. They were very small, three to four inches (or so.) They fly straight out perpendicular to the ship's course and go ten to twenty feet (or so) in the air. There were some larger ones nearer the bridge. One brilliant blue fish was just below the surface. I saw 3 other ships, mostly on the horizon. I started reading "A Tramp Abroad."

Lunch - chicken soup, grilled pork steaks, mashed potatoes, melon, flan. Back in my cabin I had a glass of wine, read a bit, and napped.

> [Napping will become a theme. Most days at sea, I took a nap of 2 to 3 hours in the afternoon. Partly to rest and relax – which is mostly what the trip was about, but partly to help the time go.]

Supper, lamb steaks (fatty,) roast potatoes. We got to Savannah in the evening once again, going up a long channel to the container port. As we entered the harbor, a helicopter hovered over us for some time, shining a floodlight down on the water around us. I wondered if they were looking for stowaways in the water having jumped off our ship.

We went up through Savannah proper at night, very scenic. Floating up the river through downtown Savannah was informative as to how high were really were off the water. There was an eight story hotel near the river edge, and we were looking down on its roof garden. Savannah looked very nice at night. If I were the sort, I would probably call it "romantic." There seemed to be a lot of amenities by the river bank due, no doubt, to massive recovery at some point. I'm sure that there must have been a time when it was all collapsed piers and industrial runoff.

The World. Around it. On a ship. Mostly.

We continued past downtown and went under a nicely-lighted modern bridge into the container port and tied up. Bedtime.

Day 10 (5) 6/21/2016 Tuesday

N32° 07.730' W81° 08.397'

At Savannah container port. Sunny, in the 70s. I got a cab at approximately 9 AM to do some more shopping, as it might have been the last chance. The driver took me to several stores for general supplies and to a pawnshop where I found a black Fender acoustic FA-100 guitar for $100. (I later Googled it – it sells retail for about $150.) It looked almost new, and the action was OK. It came with bag, a spare set of strings, a tuner, a strap and a wrench. Factory stuff. It seemed to tune OK and play just fine, although the bottom E string thumped a bit. No big deal. Got back to the ship by 10:30 AM. The Cab cost $40.00. Lunch was roast chicken and mashed potatoes.

The usual loading and unloading had gone on, of course, and any negligible "view" that I might have had out my front windows was at that point absolutely gone.

Max was gone. Probably there would be no other passengers for balance of trip. I heard my first announcement over the intercom. Didn't understand a word. I hoped it hadn't concerned me.

Supper – beef – sort of like carne asada but not spicy, and orange rice. I went up top again to see us cast off. We went very slowly at first as other ships were being maneuvered downstream. There was good light for pictures of the river and bridge. I took pictures of people at the riverside watching us, taking pictures and waving. Lots of bars and restaurants by the river side in Savannah. I waved. Yuri, the First Officer, came out and waved, resplendent in uniform. We were quite the attraction, which was no wonder as we must have looked huge to the people on the riverside. We must have been quite impressive from ground level. At one point along by riverfront bars and restaurants I heard a trumpet playing "God Bless America."

The World. Around it. On a ship. Mostly.

Max had said I should take his remaining water bottles from his cabin once he was gone. I did, and nicked his bathmat as well.

The World. Around it. On a ship. Mostly.

Day 11 (6) 6/22/2016 Wednesday

N32° 25.894' W79° 31.285'

Up at 6 AM. About 30 miles outside of Charleston, not moving. Charleston had not been on our original schedule. We learned of its addition while we were in Newark. No cause to be upset, as this sort of thing is common with freighter travel. They have a schedule, but it is, as we will continue to see, subject to change based on economics, politics and typhoonery.

Had my usual breakfast. I gave steward his first tip. I meant to do it weekly on Wednesdays at breakfast time, and remembered to do it every week.

> [One tips one's Steward. One tips nobody else, as he not only serves at meals but makes up the room. About that – every other day he came in in the late morning to make the bed and tidy generally. On Sundays he changed the sheets. I tipped well. I won't mention the amount, but various guides I had read suggested a range of dollar amounts per day, and I went for the upper amount. I tipped weekly, instead of waiting until the end like on a cruise ship. This seemed to make Marco happy. Sometimes he would leave tins of shortbreads in my cabin.]

Went up to the bridge. Ivan said we weren't moving because we were waiting for a favorable tide in Charleston. I had not realized how important tides still are to ships.

We expected to be at the Charleston Pilot Point at about 1600 hours.

> [The "Pilot Point" is the place where the Harbor Pilot, at great risk of being drowned or crushed against the side of the ship, jumps off the little Pilot Boat onto a ladder hanging from our ship. He then would guide us into port. He does this several times a day, both getting onto ships to take them in and getting off of ships that he's taken out of port. He's gotta be either crazy or very well paid. I became a bit fascinated with pilot boats on the trip. I would often wait until late at night in the pitch-dark bridge until the Pilot either arrived or left. As thrilling as it was to watch him

jump from ship to boat or the reverse in daylight, it was like a circus act at night. I was starting to get used to nautical terms by this time. I put in "1600 hours" to show off. It's 4:00 PM]

Marco brought a can of Folgers coffee (regular) to my cabin. Funny how a couple of days ago there was no non-instant caffeinated ground coffee on board and now, post-tip, there is. Also – he's here and giving the bathroom a thorough scrub-out. I sat out on "porch" outside my porthole. I made a note to go out there with my iPod and noise-canceling headset soon. 9:30-ish (AM) we started to move toward Charleston.

Lunch – something wrapped in a sort of hard tortilla (schwarma) containing traces of chicken, chopped onions and peppers, french fries and who knows what, slathered with mayonnaise. A sort of stale leftovers burrito. Good pork meatball soup, though,

The Chief Engineer asked if I have ever crossed the equator on a ship before. I wondered if there might be some goings-on for those of us crossing the Equator by ship for the first time.

[There weren't]

I asked the C.E. about the ports we would visit in Asia. He said that we would dock at a port in Shanghai that is close to town. Kuala Lumpur is 2 or 3 hours from the port. For Vietnam, I have to ask captain to arrange a shore pass 3-4 days in advance, though we may only be in port 8 or so hours. Hong Kong should be OK for a visit.

Into Charleston harbor. Saw Ft. Sumter in the harbor and tried to visualize the battle. It would have helped if I had known where they were shelled from. Must google that. We went by just as they were lowering the flag for the evening.

We went by an aircraft carrier tied up along the shore. It is there as a museum. I googled it post-trip and it's the "Yorktown."

The World. Around it. On a ship. Mostly.

Lots of boats in the river, and up-river there were rich people's houses with large private boat docks and large private boats. At the end of one such pier there was a boathouse that had in it a dining table with 8 chairs. Fancy. Again, we sailed up a river channel through town, under a high bridge, and into the container port.

Supper – same soup, chicken "tepanyaki" – stirfry chicken with peppers, onions and carrots. Not bad. Something like a potato pancake along side. Very sleepy in the evening. Probably to do with all the time outside in the wind and sun.

The World. Around it. On a ship. Mostly.

Day 12 (7) 6/23/2016 Thursday

N32° 39.206' W79° 39.995'

Speed 13 kn Heading 120^0

> [The speed and heading numbers are courtesy of the GPSTest app on my phone.]

The weather continued to be very nice, sunny and mild. It was a pleasure, and still a novelty to, when far from land, see a full circle of horizon in the sunshine, with very few clouds. There was enough wind to kick up whitecaps on the surface, and they sparkled in the sun. At this point, seeing another ship or the shore was not such a thrill as it would become after weeks (literally) at sea with no sight of land or other vessels.

We left Charleston early, while I was asleep. It was the first day of the Atlantic crossing. Finally done messing about in American ports. I sent my first status report home after breakfast, then up to the bridge. I talked with Ivan about the "slop chest" and got the list of items available.

He said we may be in Port Kelang (Malaysia) long enough to visit Kuala Lumpur. We'll see, there's lots of time to think about that.

Bowling along at up to 16 knots. (18.4125 MPH.)

Lunch – 2 stuffed peppers. There was a bowl of salad! Lettuce and chopped tomatoes, green peppers, tomatoes and cucumbers. The steward asked me if I liked this. Apparently the officers don't. He gestured toward the empty officers' table and said "They no like – sliced." We must have taken on fresh vegetables at one of the last stops. We'll see how long they last.

> [I started to notice a certain tightening of food items as we went farther and farther on this leg. Remember, we were crossing the Atlantic at an angle, going around the tip of Africa, across the Indian Ocean at an angle, and would go a bit farther yet before we would have a chance to re-supply.]

Also, after lunch he brought me a chocolate ice cream bar and said "Sabana." Apparently we took on frozen items in Savannah. Napped 1:00-3:00 PM.

I took my folding chair (provided with the room) out onto the porch and found a shady spot. Plugged headphones into iPod. Noise-canceling seemed to work pretty well, but the iPod didn't. Nathan shakin'. Brought it in to charge it and see what would happen. Interesting that, when I realized it wasn't working, I sat there anyway and watched the water. When I got back in I had been out for about an hour – slightly over. Didn't seem that long. The iPod seems to be charging.

Supper – grilled boneless chicken breast, roasted potatoes, salad(!). There were only cruets of vinegar and olive oil for salad dressing, but that would do. At lunch and supper there was always good French bread and now, real butter. There was also usually cheese – swiss, a sort of bleu cheese variety and some sort of brie-like cheese. All good.

The kitchen staff (and steward – which is good as it kept him from hovering) were following some sort of game in the pantry. Soccer? From the sound, it seemed to be on TV(?). The announcer was very excited, and it seemed to be in English. I guess there are a couple of championships going on, but how do they get TV reception? Wondered – why didn't I bring a bunch of DVDs? I brought one, so I knew I could play them, but why not bring the Marx Brothers set, for example? Oh, well. Made decaf in my room so it wouldn't keep me up (7 PM). Watched some Dr. Who and turned in around 9:30

First email home:

[These emails will, as a rule, be as I sent them at the start of the day. Sometimes the email will express an expectation that will have been contradicted in the daily entry, which tells about the day as it happened, after I sent the email. Should I have put the

The World. Around it. On a ship. Mostly.

emails before the daily entries? Maybe, but I am pretty sure that my readers can deal with it. Perhaps they'll even get a chuckle at seeing just how wrong I sometimes was, or shed a tear over how hopeful I had been, only to see my hopes dashed. Any kick you get out of it is fine with me.]

We have departed Charleston, our third and final eastern-seaboard stop after leaving Newark, and are heading across the Atlantic. Time for a status report. I was disappointed that we are not going through Gibraltar, the Mediterranean, and the Suez Canal, but going around "The Horn of Africa" has, as has been pointed out, its own romance. I will still at some point get in touch with the cruise agency, at least to tell them that they need to update their brochure. With the addition of Charleston, the ports of call are anticipated to still be the same, and the trip is not anticipated to take much, if any, longer. We are at this point about 2 days behind schedule.

The ship is, for the most part, highly industrial. Having said that, of course, the cabin and the "Castle" are clean and pleasant, and run a bit like a B & B (as far as passengers are concerned) that also serves lunch and supper. But if one wants to go out onto the

The World. Around it. On a ship. Mostly.

main deck (what there is of it) one must at least put on a hard-hat. The outside areas in the castle have no such requirement. It is possible to go all the way to the bow and stern. Actually, the bow area is rather pleasant. All that is there are the winches for the anchors (2) and for the tying-off ropes. It is very quiet, being as far away from the engine as possible. There is a substantial wall of hull making it hard to see out, but also hard to fall overboard. The stern is larger, dirtier and covered over. Over the railings at the stern (which are lowest down to the water level), there are orange plastic guards designed to make it impossible for a grappling-hook to grab on. An anti-piracy measure. The entire rest of the deck is a mass of containers, stacked from far below the deck to far above. I was given a safety orientation and tour by the Safety Officer which included not only getting into the lifeboat, but getting a briefing as to how to drive it.

The officers are all Eastern European, speaking different degrees of English. The crew are

The World. Around it. On a ship. Mostly.

all Philipino, with the exception of one Philipina, a young woman who works in the engine room. Everyone is quite pleasant. The steward who looks after the rooms (Officers and passengers) is very nice, but speaks less English than anyone else. The Officers' Mess is pleasant, with a table that seats 6, and another that seats 4, for the officers. I have seldom seen more than one or two of them there at a time. The steward will, at a certain point, put plates at their places covered with plastic wrap for them to microwave when they come off shift and want lunch or supper.

Passengers have their own table, a bit off to the side. In the corner there is a spiral staircase that leads up to the Officer's Lounge, which looks very much like what I suppose a frat house rec room would look like, and seems mostly to be used for playing Nintendo or whatever. Except for the "Master" (Captain), the officers are all young men in their late 20s to early 30s. As a rule, except when in port, they wear mostly shorts and t-shirts.

The World. Around it. On a ship. Mostly.

So far, I spend time in my cabin, reading and writing up a daily log, napping and generally pottering about. I go up to the bridge (usually the outside "wings" either side of it - no hard-hat required) to have a look around. So far, mostly horizon and sea. A few ships. An oil rig or two (we're fairly coastal up to now) and sometimes flying fish. In the bridge, and down at main deck level in an office (oddly enough, that level is called the "Upper Deck") there is a board where they post time in port, "shore leave" hours, etc. We found out in Norfolk that those hours can change. When we went to into town (Wal-Mart) to pick up misc. stuff, we were told to be back by 2:00 pm. After we were there, and had gone our separate ways, they stared calling us from the ship to say that now we were due back by 12:30 instead. Quite a scramble to get back.

I expect I will use the gym - where they have a treadmill and stationary bike - at some point. There is an "Indoor pool" about 10 feet square which they will at some point fill with sea water.

The World. Around it. On a ship. Mostly.

I'll probably try that out too. I've done one load of laundry – not easy with unfamiliar front-loaders with enigmatic, European-style instructions. It seemed to work, however.

I've been arranging my environment. The small bookshelf now has my books on it, I've magnet-clipped a large world map to the steel wall by the desk to mark our daily position, I've covered the picture on the wall (of another of their ships) with a Cornish flag and – thanks to the bedding department at Wal-Mart, have put a mattress topper on the bed, which has the native softness of asphalt. I discovered in the tiny "Passenger Recreation Room" a drip coffee maker, with a UK-style plug (which means that it will work on the ship's 220 volt current,) and I moved it to my room. It works just fine with my plug adaptor (as does everything else electronic and electric so far). Picked up some Maxwell House and I'm good to go for making my own coffee. Also in the passengers' rec room there is a mini-fridge of a different brand than the not-very-cold one in the

The World. Around it. On a ship. Mostly.

room. The rec room fridge also makes ice! Since I am the only passenger, that room is a sort of annex to my room. I will probably use it sometimes, if only to get a change of scene. I have availed myself, on shore excursions, of a moderate supply of spirits which should make the trip a bit smoother. I also found that the room fridge is just right, size and temperature-wise, for a wine box. So I don't seem too depraved, look at a world map and trace the route from Charleston SC to Port Kelang Malaysia and see if it's unreasonable that I might want a toddy or two en-route. If I don't have it now, I won't be able to get it for over a month (that applies to everything.) No spirits are available on the ship, as it turns out.

I bought a guitar at a pawn shop in Savannah. A black Fender Acoustic 6-string.

I'm sure that as I watch the weeks go by with nothing to look at but horizon, I will wonder what I'm doing out here. I do miss you all, and am trying not to get too homesick. Also, at some point down around South Africa, I'm told

The World. Around it. On a ship. Mostly.

that the sea will get pretty rough, so some stark terror should break up the monotony.

There was another passenger until Savannah, where he got off. A retired guy named Max who was very friendly and showed me the ropes to a large degree. (Max was very careful to let me know that his net worth is 8 million and that he owns both a Mercedes and a BMW. And a boat. And a pool. In a gated community in Florida. He would want me to pass that on to you. A nice guy really, but he is just a bit impressed with himself.) It's probably as well that he's gone. We talked briefly about politics earlier, and he bemoaned that Trump was the likely Republican candidate. He then said, "I'll vote for him, though – I'm a Republican." I pointed out that he didn't have to, but we might have argued about that sort of thing. As far as I know, no other passengers are expected for the remainder of the trip.

One young officer has already opened the subject of the Cold War. Interesting discussions to follow, I expect.

The World. Around it. On a ship. Mostly.

If anybody goes over to my place, could you see if I remembered to put the can of coffee into the freezer? I think that I forgot. Could you put it in? Thanks.

Sorry that I can't send pictures. I can't receive them either, sadly. I'm sure I'll have access to pictures, especially of Grandkids, after I get back.

The World. Around it. On a ship. Mostly.

Day 13 (8) 6/24/2016 Friday

N29° 48.024' W73° 41.527'

Speed 16 kn Heading 120°

403 miles from yesterday's position. Av. Speed last 24 hours – 16 kn. 1146 miles from home.

Smooth sea, some clouds. The sea was so smooth, in fact, that you could see the few clouds that there were perfectly reflected on the surface, mirror-like. It was the first day entirely away from land (we started from Charleston the day before). It must have rained the previous night – it was wet on deck and on top of the containers. A change in vibration woke me up. I kept dreaming that I was teaching an HTML class.

> [Before I retired, I used to teach people how to use computers.]

I had started measuring distance traveled since the last mark (the day before), and how far I was from home, partly because I found out how to measure in BaseCamp, and partly to see when the "miles from home" number would start getting lower. I measured 9870 miles from home when I was in South Australia a couple of years ago – wouldn't be topping that, I bet. I looked at our progress down the coast of Africa (Which was still far to the east. We were much closer to South America) – we were already slightly south of Marrakech.

The steward come in to tidy. I asked him for a fly swatter and some oil for the door hinges. He brought the swatter, but said that he would see "Dick Peters" about the oil. I was absolutely sure that there is no one named Dick Peters on the ship, so I wondered what that part will come to?

Went up to starboard (right) side bridge wing. Nothing in sight, just a few clouds. No sea can be any calmer. Other than our wake there were no little white-caps at all. Took my chair and iPod out to the porch. The noise-cancelling headset worked well. So did the iPod, this time. I listened for an hour or so. Very nice.

Lunch – beef patties and mashed potatoes and mushrooms in sauce. Salad. I began to feel like I was eating too much and should cut down.

I drafted an email to the agent concerning the misinformation about the route in their on-line brochure. It's pretty strong, and I should sit on it a bit before sending.

Supper – 2 pieces of pizza – surprisingly not bad – and salad. Went down to passenger recreation room. There was better light there for reading, I discovered. Today I finished "A Tramp Abroad" and started "Golden Spiders."

The World. Around it. On a ship. Mostly.

Day 14 (9) 6/25/2016 Saturday

N26° 18.608' W67° 17.147'

Speed 16 kn Heading 122°

459 miles from yesterday's position. Av. Speed last 24 hr – 19 kn. 1591 miles from home.

I woke at 5am with vertigo. (No, I had not hit the whisky the night before.) I got up and went to the bathroom, but experienced no nausea and it passed off after a while. The inner ear finally freaking out a bit from the constant pitching and rolling? I still felt it a little when I lay back down and when I rolled over. Later in the morning I still felt a bit off. It was a touch of some sort of seasickness, I suppose. Took a Dramamine.

> [That was the only bit of what might be a sort of seasickness that I had on the trip. I'm not bragging about being immune, and it's more due to the ship, even lacking stabilizers, being very stable and not given to violent motion, even in high seas.]

The ship was rocking a bit more – still pretty slight. The engine was vibrating more than usual, and pulsing.

Looked at the map – we were as far south as Miami and eastward about halfway across Maine. Compared to Africa – ¾ of the way down Morocco.

Breakfast – 1 egg, 1 piece of bacon, 1 slice of toast. No nausea, some veritigo. Napped most of the morning.

Lunch was white bean soup, grilled ham slices and, on the same plate, green salad with canned tuna. I had already served myself some salad, so I got my leafy greens that day. Steward said "Party tonight – D deck - 6:00." I wondered what that would be. Supper included, I presumed. He said "good pah-tee" while making the so-so waggle with his hand.

Next – laundry. I saw first officer going into laundry room and checked to see if a machine was available. He had both washers going, so I waited.

On the bridge I had a chat with the new Captain (The other one left us in Savannah). I sat on a cabinet – he had them bring me a chair. He said we'd probably get to Port Kelang on July 26 – in almost exactly 1 month to the day. He said we should have a week or so of good weather, then maybe rougher seas – definitely rougher around Africa. We talked about different air, different stars in Southern Hemisphere. He showed me charts of the route through Japan – between Hokkaido and Honshu – about 10 miles apart at the narrowest. Good picture opportunity.

The First Officer's laundry was still in machine. I would do mine tomorrow. Napped a bit – still some vertigo. I hope it goes away.

The party turned out to be a barbecue, on the outside of D deck where there is more outside deck room. There were several trays of uncooked meat – some marinated – and 2 grills. One got one's meat and grilled it oneself. The Chief Engineer, in true engineer fashion, sort of took charge of grilling. There was also orange rice, garlic bread, chips, pop etc. It all tasted good. There was a lot of wind and engine noise, as well as what seemed to be eastern European covers of American pop tunes ("Nothing's Gonna Stop Us Now") from a CD player. I had a good appetite, although I didn't pig out.

Got to admit that the vertigo had me worried. I supposed it was a form of seasickness and would pass, but, of course, I also formed worst-case scenarios. Got a bit of the what-the-hell-am-I-doing-out-here, I guess. And a bit scared that things were going to get worse. Not really prepared for the reality of sea-travel, perhaps. I hoped the next day would be better. No drink at bedtime, a Dramamine instead.

The World. Around it. On a ship. Mostly.

Day 15 (10) 6/26/2016 Sunday

N22° 31.022' W61° 18.683'

Speed 17 kn Heading 125°

458 miles from yesterday's position. Av. Speed last 24 hr – 19 kn. 2047 miles from home.

Continued good weather. Warm, breezy and very sunny. Slight vertigo but much better than the day before – cross fingers.

Progress down Africa – past Morocco, just north of the border between Western Sahara and Mauritania.

I saw a white ship on the horizon. It didn't look like a ship at first, just a big white cube. Through binoculars it looked like a light blue container ship with huge white bales of something stacked up instead of containers. Whatever it was was very tall and seemed to bulge beyond sides of ship. It seemed to be heading toward Haiti or Venezuela. Ivan said it was likely a liquid gas carrier.

I had a look at the crew list and pictures, which was posted in the office. Our new "master" has a name (which I can't tell you – but it would be something like "Captain Zap" or "Captain Eternity" or some such) that would make a good comic book character, and is somewhat formal and imperious, definitely "in charge" but gracious and accommodating.

I started my laundry. I made different guesses as to what the controls mean this time. I was interested to see how it would come out.

Visited bridge and chatted with Ivan, the Third Officer. The First Officer came by and gave me more operational and safety tips – nothing new. Ivan said we may be getting another passenger in Hong Kong.

Lunch was steak (probably leftover from barbecue yesterday,) fries and broccoli. There was salad. And an ice cream bar. Laundry came out OK. Napped.

At 5:07 I looked out and even though the sky was fairly bright, it was raining.

Excitement! The fire alarm went off, and I dutifully went to the bridge.

> [We had several fire drills and one evacuation drill, but this was the only actual emergency. Guess where the fire was!]

It turned out that in the fluorescent light fixture just above my bed something had started smoking. I had no suspicion at that time that the problem was right there in my room. I didn't smell smoke until I went out into the hallway, as the smoke had gone up into the ceiling and out toward the hall, where the smoke detector picked it up.

After a while I asked the bridge crew if it was OK to go down to my cabin, and they said yes. I found just about all of the officers clustered around my door, with a ceiling panel out. They had used the fire extinguisher. All was OK at that point, and an electrician arrived to replace the burned-out element in the light. Lesson – don't leave things lying around I wouldn't want the crew to see. Fortunately I hadn't. They told me that the power would be off in my cabin for a while, and the Captain invited me back to the bridge where he made espresso and gave me further seamanship lessons. I now think I know the difference between waves and swell. He said that waves up to 5 meters were no big deal. That's over 30-foot waves!

Supper – lasagna – not too bad. Back at my cabin there was still a little smoke/electric smell. Windows were open to air the room – I closed them. Then chased flies!

The World. Around it. On a ship. Mostly.

Finished "Too Many Clients." Now I have read, and own, everything, to the best of my knowledge, that Rex Stout wrote about Nero Wolfe. I will enjoy rereading them all many times, but it's sad that I will never again read one for the first time. Thanks, Val, for getting me hooked.

Day 16 (11) 6/27/2016 Monday

N14° 30.714' W50° 24.110'

469 miles from yesterday's position. Av. Speed last 24 hr – 19 kn. 2497 miles from home.

Progress down Africa – about halfway down the coast of Mauritania. Seemed like we'd have to change clocks soon – my guess was today. Made a note to ask on the bridge. When I asked, the Captain said tomorrow. Sent the email (version 2 – toned down) to the agent regarding my disappointment over the misinformation about our route.

> [I never got a reply, and the last time I looked, the misinformation was still in their on-line brochure.]

I stopped by the "gym" and tried the treadmill. I really should have tried get down there daily, but oh, well…….

It was interesting to look out at the weather. The scope of the view is so wide that one can see whole storms, and make out clearly where it is raining. Strange to be in sunny skies and look maybe 30 miles away and see dark clouds and rain falling.

Supper was a bit of poached fish, rice (basically white fried rice with no soy sauce), and green beans with clear soy noodles. Salad.

Read some PG Wodehouse on my Kindle. Not much went on today. We continued steady on a southeast course. Played the guitar and sang a bit.

The World. Around it. On a ship. Mostly.

Day 17 (12) 6/28/2016 Tuesday

N18° 32.936' W55° 39.977'

Speed 16 kn Heading 126°

448 miles from yesterday's position. Av. Speed last 24 hr – 18 kn. 2933 miles from home.

Weather – good. The sea is slightly choppy and there are some clouds. Progress down Africa – just south of Dakar. Slept through the night all the way to the alarm – first time.

I walked out on the deck. To get to the bow or stern, one had to walk along a narrow area at the very edge of the deck, with a ceiling above made of the bottoms of containers. There are various pipes and valves and such jutting out, and sometimes I couldn't move forward without scuttling sideways. Overhead, especially in other-than-glassy seas, the containers banged and groaned, and sometimes it sounded like something inside one of them was rolling around, side to side, end to end. That couldn't have been good for the contents.

On rough days, I was not allowed out on that part of the ship at all. And any time I went out there, I had to wear a hard-hat. This time I couldn't get all the way to bow on either side due to ongoing painting. It seemed like somebody was always painting something on that ship. So I went to the stern and took pictures.

Later, on the bridge, I asked Ivan if we were listing slightly to starboard. He said "A lot! Wind."

Toward suppertime – it was heavily overcast and there'd been some rain. The weather was changing as we neared the equator. The clocks still hadn't changed, and the time on the Phone GPS still read as Eastern Time. Seemed like it should get an hour later very soon. Finally an announcement at about 6 PM – put clocks ahead one hour at midnight.

Day 18 (13) 6/29/2016 Wednesday

N10° 29.345' W45° 29.281'

Speed 16 kn Heading 130°

431 miles from yesterday's position. Av. Speed last 24 hr – 18 kn. 3369 miles from home.

Progress down Africa – about halfway down the coast of Guinea.

Mostly cloudy – smooth – looks windy.

I tipped the steward. In the room, I worked on the PowerPoint presentation I would show to the family after I got home – got it pretty much up to date. Any pictures I would take from there to South Africa would be worked in. The bow, for example, and rough weather if any. Air conditioning is a fine thing. There we were 10 degrees North of the equator and I put on socks and shoes because my feet were cold.

Just thought of something I don't want to forget. After the "fire," up on the bridge, the captain said that, when he had been an officer on cruise ships, the rule had been: "In case of fire, SMILE!" to keep the passengers from panicking.

Walked on treadmill for 30 min – 1.8 km. Should have done that at least every other day. I went up to the bridge. There was a meeting going on, so I scampered to the starboard wing. I was out there 45 min or so and watched the weather.

This time, I watched the weather come straight toward us. The dark clouds and the pillars of rain were dead-ahead. It was fascinating to see how low they actually were, and how fast we reached them. Or they reached us. Or both. Fortunately there was some shelter on the bridge wing so I didn't get soaked. I didn't

The World. Around it. On a ship. Mostly.

want to go back inside the bridge until the meeting was over. From the gestures, it was fairly intense.

The meeting was still on when I snuck by to go down to lunch. Lunch was fried shrimp, orange rice pilaf and zucchini, grilled or something.

It got rather foggy. Equatorial weather? At 4:00 we were at North 08° 42. I noticed that the distance from the east coast of the USA to southern Africa is the longest stretch of the trip, longer than crossing the Pacific. Also that just before Malaysia the distance **to** home will start getting shorter than the distance **from** home. Getting a bit homesick? Maybe, but reading a book (<u>Nimisha's Ship</u> by Anne McCaffrey) about people far from home might have something to do with it. Also the fact that in the book they kept eating hamburgers and having babies didn't help. I missed both hamburgers and the babies.

I figured I'd send an email to Sam to let him know how things are going and send him the lyrics to "Big Container" but I seem to have forgotten to bring along his email address. After supper I went to send a test email to see if what I remember is right, but someone had signed off of the computer in the office and I didn't know the password. The one scribbled on the monitor (almost illegible, but I'm pretty sure I tried all of the 4-letter combos that it might be) didn't work.

> [Sam is my "studio guy." I do music on the side, and he owns a studio in which I record, and he provides a lot of backing tracks.]

Supper – pork stirfry, roasted potatoes, some sort of sauté of shredded cabbage, onion and bits of what seemed to be sausage. Pretty good.

Finished "Nimisha's Ship" and started on "Dubliners" by James Joyce. An English professor friend said it was a good intro to Joyce, whom I'd never read. Pretty depressing at first, but I

The World. Around it. On a ship. Mostly.

carried on. Made a note to guard against melancholy and homesickness.

Email Home:

A quick update on position, since we're too far from land to be tracked. We're pretty much straight east of Trinidad/Tobago, which is just about 10 north, and, for lack of an obvious landmark, we're 45 west.

If we progress south at the same rate today and tonight, we should be at about 2 north tomorrow morning, meaning that we will cross the equator during the day. On the GPS phone app I downloaded, I can watch the numbers decline to 0 and then start up again south of the equator.

Hope all is well with all of you-

The World. Around it. On a ship. Mostly.

Day 19 (14) 6/30/2016 Thursday

N6° 08.879' W40° 25.282'

Speed 17 kn Heading 130°

455 miles from yesterday's position. Av. Speed last 24 hr – 19 kn. 3806 miles from home.

Progress down Africa – even with Abidjan, Ivory Coast

We weren't as close to the Equator as I thought we'd be in the morning. It seemed that maybe we'd cross it that night or the next morning. The weather was better. I sent our position home, and sent a test email to Sam. I hope one of the addresses I sent it to works.

We were definitely south of the Caribbean "cruise islands" and such – outside of the tourist realm and into open ocean, at the narrowest part of the Atlantic. If the two plates reversed direction and South America and Africa started getting closer again, we'd have to hurry to get out of the way or be crushed between. There would be stretches of wide-open ocean farther south in the Atlantic, in the Indian and in the Pacific. But we were several hundred miles from Brazil, and farther from Africa. That was open ocean enough for me.

Did a half-hour on the treadmill while the steward made up the room. Used the headphones and iPod. Good plan? Seemed like it. I had pulled the last 3 bottles of water out of the case and put the empty case by the trash can. The steward left a new case. I hoped that would keep up. Just at 5:00 I heard the clock start clicking like it did the other day when the time zone changed. Sure enough it went from 5 to 6. I checked on the bridge to be sure it was right. No announcement. I made a note to be alert to these time changes.

Supper – deep-fried calamari – looked like onion rings. Also rice pilaf and some sort of rolled up fried wonton.

The World. Around it. On a ship. Mostly.

Email Home:

Just another position update-

N6° 08 W40° 25

For a north-south reference, we're about even with Abidjan, Ivory Coast. For an east-west reference, we're halfway between Sao Luis and Fortaleza, Brazil. In another day or two, we may be close enough to Brazil for the tracking site to pick us up - give it a try.

How are the Cubs doing?

The World. Around it. On a ship. Mostly.

Day 20 (15) 7/1/2016 Friday

N1° 57.211' W35° 38.974'

Speed 16 kn Heading 128°

438 miles from yesterday's position. Av. Speed last 24 hr – 18 kn. 4261 miles from home.

Progress down Africa – Halfway down the coast of Equatorial Guinea.

The weather was foggy and the sea a bit rough. The fog settled right down on the water, and reduced our circle of view from a diameter of maybe 30 miles to a couple hundred yards. Thankfully radar can still see miles out.

We were halfway down Africa – my Medicare part B kicked in that day – all was well! I gave my phone alarm clock a rest last night, as the phone seemed to be getting warm, maybe from being on charge all the time. I unplugged it to give it a chance to discharge a bit and used the kindle as an alarm. I almost missed breakfast (well – not really, but I slept nearly an hour late, rising at about 6:45 rather than 6) as the Kindle didn't seem to have gotten set to the new time. I was sure I'd done it – oh, well.

It was the day to cross the Equator. It occurred to me that this trip was already longer (in time, not quite in distance yet) than the trip from New York to Southampton on the Queen Mary 2, even if you disregard the days on the eastern seaboard. Not significant, but interesting.

Lunch – roast chicken, mashed potatoes, oxtail soup.

Supper – lamb chops and roast potatoes.

We crossed the Equator at 6:45 PM. I stood on the port-side bridge wing and watched the numbers on the GPS go down in the fading light. They hit zero and then started up again, with an "S." I was in the Southern Hemisphere again!

The World. Around it. On a ship. Mostly.

Day 21 (16) 7/2/2016 Saturday

S1° 58.922' W31° 16.173'

Speed 16 kn Heading 128°

405 miles from yesterday's position. Av. Speed last 24 hr – 16 kn. 4663 miles from home.

Progress down Africa – 2/3 of the way down Gabon Coast.

Partly cloudy – smooth but with a bit of rocking. More rocking than most days to that point, but not anywhere near "rough." More than halfway down Africa – that was good progress. Started laundry at 8:09 AM. I noticed on a chart on the wall that the time for the wash cycle I chose (normal – cotton – 60 [believing that's 60 degrees Celsius]) will take 189 minutes – till 11:18. I wasn't sure if that's wash only or wash-rinse-spin. Made a note to check a few minutes before 11:18 and see if it's spinning. Then there's at least an hour to dry. They could use some good old USA washing machine technology! Started "Hotel Paradise."

Lunch – I saw "schwarma" on the card and groaned inwardly (that was the "leftovers burrito" from last week), but after the soup, steward brought me a grilled chicken breast and fries. He had seen that when we had schwarma before I hadn't eaten much and figured he'd bring me something I would like. He also brought some salad tongs to serve myself the salad. Very nice. Cause and effect of the tip or just a nice man? Who knew?

All it said for supper was lentil soup. Same as at lunch as usual, and I could make a meal of it. The soups usually have some nice hunks of meat in – the lentil soup had pork.

I learned by bitter experience that you have to let the washing machine count down the 2 minutes after the end after the spin before turning the dial to off, or it will never open. I ran the spin cycle again and all was well. There was a surreal moment when it played a cute little electronic tune at the moment (I assume) it unlocked the door.

Napped. It rained in the afternoon. Played guitar a bit – I want to self-teach myself some blues up the neck in A for "Big Container." I actually made a tiny bit of progress.

> [That was about the end of my self-guitar-teaching. I realized that I was merely suffering from "McGhee/Watson Envy." Every time I heard Brownie McGhee on my iPod, I wanted to play like him. Every time I heard Doc Watson, I wanted to play like him. Never, in a million years, will I be good enough to tie the shoes of either of those (late, lamented) gentlemen.]

Reading an article Alice sent about a Professor's trip on a freighter – the author visited both the Officers' and the Crews' rec rooms on the ship she took. I, on the other hand, have been asked to respect the "space" (my term) of the Officers and Crew by staying **out** of their rec rooms. The Professor – attractive young lady. I – large, fuzzy old man. Hmmmmmm…….

In the article, it talked about the author sharing a glass of wine with the officers in their lounge and then going into the crew rec room and seeing brandy and beer. Our ship was a "dry ship" and the only one allowed any alcohol at all was me, and it was limited to one glass of wine a day. I hadn't pressed the point of actually getting that wine. I'd have felt self-conscious sitting in the mess drinking it while others couldn't. I wonder if that's a difference between a British registry ship (ours is a British-Registry ship) and a French-Registry ship (the one in the article?)

Supper – some sort of pork stew. May have been a bit of kidney or liver in.

Clocks ahead at midnight.

The World. Around it. On a ship. Mostly.

Email Home:

Here's our position as of 6AM local time 7/2/16-

S1° 58.922' W31° 16.173'

Since you're copy-and-pasting the numbers into Google Maps, I've provided somewhat more detailed numbers. You see that the first letter is now "S" indicating that we did indeed cross the Equator yesterday evening.

We're relatively close to the coast of Brazil, so the ship tracker site may be able to pick us up.

Progress down Africa - 2/3 of the way down Gabon Coast. More than halfway down Africa!

Ed and Alice - thanks for the Cubs updates. I hope they're still doing well when I get back.

Mary- sorry if you didn't get the first couple of emails. I copied everybody's email addresses from my home computer, but yours must have gotten garbled. If you want me to resend the first one or two emails, please let me know. I hope this one comes through OK.

No particular news - still smooth sailing, with a bit of "rock and roll"

The World. Around it. On a ship. Mostly.

but so far no seasickness. I'm told that it will get rougher as we approach the Horn Of Africa. We'll see.
I hope all are well.
Kiss the grandkids for me!

The World. Around it. On a ship. Mostly.

Day 22 (17) 7/3/2016 Sunday

S6° 00.404' W26° 36.399'

Speed 16 kn Heading 130°

425 miles from yesterday's position. Av. Speed last 24 hr – 16 kn. 5073 miles from home.

Progress down Africa – Just south of the northern border of Angola.

The alarm went off at 6 and there was no light coming in window. Must have been because of the new time zone.

Sea smooth but not glassy. Still nothing to be called "rough." If we'd been going straight south, we'd be even with Cape Town. 17 days at sea - if this trip actually turned out to be 68 days at sea, that would have meant (68÷4=17) that we were ¼ of the way through.

I wasn't constantly looking at the sea, but I had seen very few ships. I suppose that they purposely stay separate from each other, and our viewing area was a circle that is at best 30 miles in diameter, but the sea seemed quite empty. I spent a half-hour on the treadmill while the steward changed the bed. The iPod and headphones with noise-reduction on helped that to be less tedious.

Chatted with Ivan on bridge – he said "When we get to South Africa, be careful about things which will slide around." Made a note to put my camera, etc. in drawers. Maybe put the laptop on floor?

Lunch – nice bit of filet steak. Fries (cold and bad) and corn. The steward brought in a bottle of red wine and showed it to me – said 3rd mate (Ivan) arranged it (it's part of his job as manager of the "Slop Chest") and did I want my one glass with lunch or dinner? I told him dinner. Saw Ivan just then and thanked him.

Napped. I saw another ship! Way off the stern – so odd an angle that, through the window, I could only see it with the left eye of the binoculars. Looked like a tanker of some sort as far as I could tell. It seemed to be going straight east. I went outside and got a better look, although it was hard to keep the binoculars steady in the wind. I braced them against a pipe. It definitely looked like a large tanker, maybe 10 miles away. Took the folding chair outside and sat on the porch for a while. Not too windy, depending on where you sit. It was nice to get some fresh air, but it looked like it might rain.

Supper – rigatoni in white mushroom sauce. A bit bland so I added come tabasco. It was nice that there was something as familiar as Tabasco sauce on the table, but the label had Chinese writing on it, which made it seem less "homey." Garlic bread. The steward poured my allotted glass of wine – nice and full. The wine was not bad – a French table claret. Dessert after lunch and supper had been rolls made with croissant dough with a bit of chocolate inside. Very good.

The World. Around it. On a ship. Mostly.

Day 23 (18) 7/4/2016 Monday

S10° 07.589' W21° 47.311'

Speed 16 kn Heading 130°

433 miles from yesterday's position. Av. Speed last 24 hr – 18 kn. 5525 miles from home.

Progress down Africa – halfway between Luanda and Huambo, Angola.

More than halfway to the halfway point as far as miles from home is concerned. The point where the miles to home would be getting smaller would be just before Port Kelang, per the expected route, to the north of Sumatra and then down the Strait of Melacca.

Cloudy and smooth in the morning. I was trying not to think of bratwurst and fireworks (see date above). After breakfast I went on deck, first aft and then to the bow. Walking under some of the containers, it smelled just like Ikea. If it were a ship from Sweden to somewhere, I'd guess that would be right. Or a ship from China to somewhere. But TO china and the rest of Asia? Oh, well.

Lunch was grilled chicken breast, mashed potatoes, some sort of purple coleslaw – didn't like it. Flan for "afters".

Another clock change – "1700 becomes 1800" making for an early dinner compared to lunch. Made a note to eat light. That seemed like a good thing as when I got to the mess at lunchtime and looked at the menu for the day it had something on it that I didn't recognize for supper. It looked like a French hybrid of some sort; "Something a la Somebody" and I suspect that the somebody is the cook. Who knows, it might be good.

The time change would mean an early bedtime too. Probably just as well, I hadn't napped particularly well.

Earlier on the bridge I had asked Ivan what the password was for the computer in the security office where we do email. A couple of times I'd found it logged off. On the monitor it said "Password:" and something that looked like "erez" or "orez" with a little horizontal line through the z. I had tried all of the possibilities I could think of and nothing worked. He said "It's 'crew'." I went back down. The first letter had a curlicue at the top and I pardoned myself for thinking that it was "a" an "e" or an "@". Never guessed it was a c. But the last letter was definitely a z. I typed in c-r-e-z and it worked. I'll have to investigate what the crew's language's alphabet looks like.

Supper – a small filet which when he brought the plate I thought might be veal but I'm pretty sure was pork, rice and some more of those rolled-up wontons. The name was "Varsa ala Dimitriu." I'll have to google "varsa" when I get home.

[I did – it means "If" in Turkish.]

The steward said that on his last ship, each passenger was entitled to a bottle of wine a day, not a glass (French registry?).

The World. Around it. On a ship. Mostly.

Day 24 (19) 7/5/2016 Tuesday

S13° 55.710' W17° 09.973'

Speed 15 kn Heading 125°

405 miles from yesterday's position. Av. Speed last 24 hr – 16 kn. 5922 miles from home.

Progress down Africa – about 2/3 of the way down the coast of Angola.

I noticed that we're as far south as the bits that stick up from the top of Australia. We were definitely on "the deep" between South America and Africa – nothing coastal about us at all. Hadn't been for some time, really, but it looked more like it on the map at that point. I made an appointment with the Chief Engineer to tour the engine room the next day at 9:00 AM. Partly cloudy, sea still a bit choppy, but the ride was still pretty smooth.

I realized a flaw in my markings and "average speed" figures – not all of the time periods between my 6 AM (or so) readings contained twenty-four hours, due to the time changes. Every two or three days, it was only twenty-three hours. Not a big thing, really but I must remember to take those numbers with a grain of salt. Not that one hour is a big deal at this speed.

30 min on treadmill while steward did the room. Several of my songs came up on the iPod. Not bad if I say so myself. Started to feel poetic – on the theme of – out here, with very little of my "stuff" – including people, places – what have I got? Is this a journey of self-discovery? Don't know as I meant it to be. It will be interesting to see what I discover about myself.

I noticed that when we round the horn of Africa, we'll be almost exactly as far south as Adelaide and the Copper Coast, where I was on my trip to Australia. Not as far east from Chicago as that, so not as far from home, but just as far south. Interesting.

Lunch – grilled pork steak and roasted potatoes and green beans. There was ground meat in the green beans. On this ship, even the vegetables had meat. A bowl of green salad still showed up every lunch and supper, as well as a cheese plate with some sort of bleu cheese (Roquefort?), swiss slices and a soft cheese (brie?). The soup was chicken soup with chicken in. With bones. Had a good nap.

Fire drill! I went to the bridge and the captain gave me coffee another lesson in ships, mostly having to do with the areas around Port Kelang and Singapore we would go through and why. Mostly it was about how high the stern is above the water. The lower the stern, the easier for pirates to get aboard. Our stern is fairly high, so we can go a certain route because of that. I think that was the gist.

He showed me a computer forecast of the seas. Looked like we would be sort of pushing an area of fairly calm water ahead of us around South Africa. Not really anything to do with us, just coincidence.

The waves were (according to him) 3.5 to 4 meters at that point. They were expected to stay that way around South Africa, according to the forecast. Good. They didn't look that high from my room, but the computer said 3 meters, and he said they were really a bit more. Over about 7 meters, we would have had to do something to avoid them. Those would be too high even for us.

He said something that indicated that he works mainly on the Atlantic, not the Pacific. I wonder if we will get a new Captain in Asia somewhere?

Supper was lamb stew. Not bad, but the peas were hard.

Email Home:

S13° 55.710' W17° 09.973'

The World. Around it. On a ship. Mostly.

Progress down Africa - about 2/3 of the way down the coast of Angola.

I hope the 4th of July went well. Sounds like the food was good, anyway. Again, no big news from this end. We're slowly but surely heading toward South Africa. I doubt if we will see it. We have to be within about 15 miles of something in order for it to appear over the horizon.
We see very few ships, for example, even though we're in a major shipping lane.

The sea continues pretty calm. Not for long, though, I have a feeling. It will be good to round Africa and start heading Northeast. Not halfway at that point, but a milestone. I may have mentioned that the miles to home will start being smaller than the miles from home just before Port Kelang.
That's as-the-crow-flies, of course. I noticed on the map that we're as far south as the bits that stick up from the top of Australia.

The World. Around it. On a ship. Mostly.

That's pretty far south. I'm glad
it's not South America we're going
around the end of!
Hope all is well-

The World. Around it. On a ship. Mostly.

Day 25 (20) 7/6/2016 Wednesday

S17° 50.701' W12° 05.693'

Speed 15 kn Heading 127°

431 miles from yesterday's position. Av. Speed last 24 hr – 18 kn. 6349 miles from home.

Progress down Africa – Just south of Namibia's northern border.

Once we crossed South Africa, we would have just about as many days at sea across the Indian Ocean to Kelang as we will have had from Charleston to our position.

At breakfast, I'd taken to just asking for "one and one" as that was how the steward conveyed the order to the cook. One fried egg, one slice of bacon. Plus I made myself one slice of toast.

Cloudy – sea about the same, a bit choppy. Smooth ride.

I was reading a favorite author – Rex Stout – (The Black Mountain) and found a quote appropriate to a certain candidate running for president in 2016:

"…the intolerable doctrine that man's sole responsibility is to his ego. That was the doctrine of Hitler … and Senator McCarthy; masquerading as a basis of freedom, it is the oldest and toughest of the enemies of freedom. I reject it and condemn it."

Took a tour of engine room with the chief engineer. I got rather puffed after going down and back up lots of stairs. It was very noisy, and with ear protection it was hard to hear, but I think I managed to absorb enough info and asked some semi-intelligent questions. We chatted afterward about politics and criminal justice/juries, etc. He will show me the steering gear maybe next week.

He said that if there was a pirate alert, I should go to the engine room door on the upper deck, and we would be taken to the "citadel," which was an internal room with a strong door to which the staff and passengers could go to in case of pirates. It was vitally important, he said, that everyone get in, as one hostage was as good as 30.

> [I never saw the "citadel." Most authors of this sort of thing say they were shown it and were sworn to secrecy as to its location. I never even saw it.]

He told me about two pirate attacks against ships he had been on, one time when pirates shot at his ship with rifles and another time with rocket-grenades. One grenade apparently pierced a container and exploded inside.

Lunch was "Chicken ala King" – chicken and mushrooms in a white sauce – no noodles, but roast potatoes. Pieces of pineapple for dessert.

The steward asked me if I wanted a tin of cookies in my room, I said yes, thanks, and found it there when I went up after lunch. He had taken it up during lunch – a fresh tin. Again – was he looking for ways to keep the tips coming (tipped him this AM) or is he just nice? I'll never know, I expect. He put it inside the cabin, answering the question of whether he could get in anytime he liked. He could.

Napped. Opened cookies. Tasty, but with a noticeable chemicalish smell, reminiscent of exhaust. I left the can open to let it dissipate if possible.

Announcement: 1700 will become 1800. We've been on GMT or whatever they changed it to for a day or so, and now we've gone the other side of it.

The World. Around it. On a ship. Mostly.

Day 26 (21) 7/7/2016 Thursday

S21° 22.688' W7° 09.665'

Speed 15 kn Heading 120^0

397 miles from yesterday's position. Av. Speed last 24 hr – 17 kn. 6772 miles from home.

Progress down Africa – Just over 1/3 down Namibia.

Somewhat more "rock and roll" overnight – slept ok, no vertigo.

Like when we were approaching the equator, we seem to slow down as we get closer to South Africa. On the 20th I would have sworn we'd be nearly there on the 22nd, but now it looks more like 5 days. Frustrating.

Cloudy. Sea smoother-looking than I would have expected considering the increased rocking, but I suspected that the waves (or swell) were higher than they looked. Also, once you get a ship this size swaying, I suppose that it takes a long time for it to slow down.

Just before 9:00 am, I got a call to come up to the bridge. I wondered what I had done wrong – felt like I was being called to the principal's office. The captain told me that in a few minutes there would be a fairly realistic drill, and I should come to the bridge and stay there for the duration. Back to my cabin. About 5 minutes later, the fire alarm went and the Captain made a "Dees ees a Dreel - Dees ees a Dreel - Dees ees a Dreel" announcement. I went to the bridge.

The Captain was coordinating a simulated fire in a container, an injured person and a stowaway all at once. I sat over to the side and stayed quiet and out of the way. It took about an hour and a quarter all told. Very interesting. At one point the captain took pains to point out to me that the clipped, simplistic way he spoke in English on the walkie/talkie to his subordinates in directing the drill did not represent his command of English. I assured him that I knew that he was much more fluent than that.

A couple of them seem concerned that I realize how fluent they are in English. And they are, for people who aren't living in an English-speaking country. If they came to Chicago to live, within a year they would be much smoother and using idioms.

During the drill, they referred to an emergency service in Rome and, I think, actually called there. At one point on the squawk box, I heard an American accent (Navy?). I hope very much that nothing like that drill actually happens.

Lunch – pork on skewers with onion and green pepper. Mashed potatoes. Ice cream bar. I checked out the "Library" again – just nautical reference books and records. Nothing to read in there. Napped. I found myself feeling a bit homesick. I looked at the grandkids' pictures, which made it both better and worse.

Supper – "beef cutlet" which is like carne asada but not as flavorful, boiled potatoes, and boiled cabbage with sausage in. I realized that starting Sunday, with Outlook in month view, I would be able to see all of the rest of the days of the trip (through Aug 20) on one screen. These little things bring the remaining time into focus and make it not seem so endless.

Email Home:

```
S21° 22.688' W7° 09.665'
Progress down Africa - Just over
1/3 down Namibia
No news, of course - we started
rocking and rolling a bit more
last night, but so far, no
seasickness or vertigo. I slept
ok. Still a few days till South
Africa, but, as I said, it looked
```

The World. Around it. On a ship. Mostly.

like we might not encounter the worst seas possible down there. Fingers crossed. When we pass South Africa, even though it won't yet be the halfway point, it will feel less like we're getting farther from our point of departure, and more like we're getting closer to our destination. Tomorrow we will (I think) have got to 1/3 of our expected days at sea.
Hope all is well there-

The World. Around it. On a ship. Mostly.

Day 27 (22) 7/8/2016 Friday

S25° 03.916' W1° 30.619'

Speed 15kn Heading 122°

430 miles from yesterday's position. Av. Speed last 24 hr – 18 kn. 7176 miles from home.

Progress down Africa – About 2/3 of the way down Namibia.

At 8:00 AM it was solid overcast. The sea was fairly smooth with some whitecaps and the ride was smooth. To date, 1/3 of the way through our expected 68 days at sea. When we "Round the Horn," it will feel like a real milestone. 30 minutes on treadmill while the steward made up the room.

Lunch – shrimp with heads on. Not a favorite, but I managed. Also fried rice and some sort of sashimi on the side. Tried the fish – not very fresh.

Napped. Worked on the PowerPoint. Lost another hour; "1700 will become 1800. Good appetite and good evening."

Supper – roast duck. Not as glamorous as it sounds.

The World. Around it. On a ship. Mostly.

Day 28 (23) 7/9/2016 Saturday

S28° 17.380' E4° 01.598'

Speed 17kn Heading 122°

405 miles from yesterday's position. Av. Speed last 24 hr –17kn. 7602 miles from home.

Progress down Africa – South border of Namibia.

Once again, as we approached something it seemed to recede. The day before I would have sworn that we would be just about at Cape Town the next morning, but Monday became likelier. Weird. Time for laundry. I hoped that this time I'll get the procedures 100% correct.

At 8:30 AM it was completely overcast and the sea was very smooth, with few whitecaps. I looked at the original schedule from the agent. It said we're supposed to hit Port Kelang, Malaysia on forty-third day at sea. Actually, that looked plausible. Rough as-the-crow-flies estimate showed us getting there on day 37, and it was bound to take longer than that – so day 43 at that point it seemed not impossible.

10:10am. Felt slightly ill. Not nauseous, just "off." I took a Dramamine just in case it was seasickness. Odd – the sea was no rougher than previously. I decided to see what would happen. No vertigo in evidence. There were twinges of a sort of "freak-out" feeling at the edges. Confinement? General anxiety? Not a good feeling. At 11:13 I felt a bit better – maybe the Dramamine kicked in? I wasn't sure I'd go down for lunch. I did anyway.

Lunch – just had some soup (tomato) and brought back a couple of bread rolls in case I'm hungry later. I copied all of the emails sent and received so far onto a thumb drive. Crossed fingers that the soup would stay down. Napped.

The World. Around it. On a ship. Mostly.

The nap seemed to go ok. I ate the bread rolls. We'll see what happens.

The menu for supper just said "Burger." I expected high comedy.

I finally mastered the laundry room. I ruled the spin-dry!

In the afternoon, I felt better, but sleepier than usual. I understand that sleepiness is one form that seasickness can take. The sea was smoother and the overcast was breaking up. I hoped for a clear night while we're this far south to look at stars. It would be good to see the Southern Cross again.

On the way to supper, waiting for the elevator on F deck which is just outside the door of the young lady of the engine room, I heard her playing a very badly tuned guitar and singing.

Supper was a sort of hamburger. It was slathered with a sauce. Not bad – not just mayo. But next time I'll see if I can get it without sauce. Might be ok. No fries or anything with it, and the meat was some sort of "Burger Mix."

I got my guitar out – sang some old Dylan songs and John Barleycorn. I was glad I brought the lyrics folder.

The World. Around it. On a ship. Mostly.

Day 29 (24) 7/10/2016 Sunday

S31° 31.521' E10° 26.340'

Speed 17kn Heading 122°

448 miles from yesterday's position. Av. Speed last 24 hr –18kn. 8065 miles from home.

Progress down Africa – Halfway down west coast of South Africa.

The sea and the ride – fairly smooth. Less choppiness, more large swells. The view would be clear once the mist went. 30 minutes on the treadmill while the steward made up the room.

Went to the bridge – saw a school of tuna jumping on the starboard side. I took a couple pictures and was going to take a video, but I ran out of battery. I didn't have spare with me. A lesson to be learned there? It was nice and cool on the starboard wing. It was winter down there, of course.

Lunch – steak, very overdone fries, a small cob of corn and an ice cream bar.

Napped. I was thinking about the length of our Atlantic crossing. Mark Twain (I'd been reading his travel books) crossed the Pacific from San Francisco to, I think, Sydney. The distance we'll have come on the Atlantic is longer. Our 7689 miles (approximately) to his 7433. There are only a few places where you can sail on one heading for this long without running into a continent or something.

I went back on the bridge in the PM. Port side. Nice and cool. Saw a couple more tuna. The 2nd officer said we'd be passing Capetown about 8:00 tomorrow, twenty-some miles away.

Supper – elbow macaroni with a red meat sauce. It also contained slices of the sausage that we established was basically a hot dog. So it was "Pasta A la Sheldon." Not bad, actually. I got my wine allotment (1 glass per day) at supper (my choice) and I usually finished supper with a piece of French bread and some cheese, with the wine. Highly civilized!

I'm finally getting the hang of taking sunset pictures on the open sea. They can be quite spectacular, with bands of red and gold at the dark grey horizon. Between the bands can be rolling spirals of gold and red which remind me of the shape of some the clouds in pictures of the planet Jupiter. The disc of the sun starts as gold and deepens to hot-coal red, often with stripes of cloud crossing it as accents. Quite beautiful.

```
Email Home:
S31° 31.521' E10° 26.340'
Hi all-
Now - or soon - you should be able
to pick us up on the Ship Locator
site.
We're getting nearer land.
Tomorrow we should wake up near
Cape Town. We won't see any of
it, of course. We would have to
be within 12 - 15 miles in order
to see it. I expect we may see
more ships. But we will be taking
a dogleg left and heading East,
then Northeast. It will, as I may
have said, feel like we've stopped
departing from our point of origin
and will be approaching our
destination. Still a long way to
go, but it will be a milestone.
There won't (I think) be as long
an unbroken string of days at sea.
Both the Indian and Pacific oceans
```

The World. Around it. On a ship. Mostly.

are big, but crossing the Atlantic on the diagonal makes it REALLY big. No news - just routine eating, reading, exercising (a little) and hanging around the ship. Mom will forward a more informative email I sent to her - thinking that I was sending it to all - with a more detailed idea of how things are on board ship.

The World. Around it. On a ship. Mostly.

Day 30 (25) 7/11/2016 Monday

S34° 29.493' E17° 30.241'

Speed 17kn Heading 117°

451 miles from yesterday's position. Av. Speed last 24 hr –18kn. 8495 miles from home.

Progress down Africa – Going around the sticky-downy bit at the southern tip.

At 6:30 am we were just going around Cape Town and would be heading east under the tip of Africa pretty much all day. Ride was smooth at that moment. The Captain's forecast of smoother-than-normal water around here seems to be holding true so far.

> [I discovered that dawns at sea can be photogenic as well. Usually more misty than sunset, but with similar colors of blazing sun and blue-grey sky. When the light is right, and the sea is calm, the surface of the sea looks like slate. Flat, hard and with a bit of patterned texture. It's often that smoky slate-grey as well. If anyone wants a picture of the sea at dawn (with or without ships in the shot) let me know. I've got hundreds.]

I realized that the constant motion, vibration, etc. reminded me a bit of living on the bus all those years ago. More room in my cabin, though, and no stagehands snoring a couple of feet away.

> [Many years ago, I worked as a stagehand on "Bus and Truck" touring companies of musicals and "legit" plays. We lived for months at a time on a bus outfitted with bunks, and were constantly swaying, bumping, stopping and starting. Actually, the ship was smoother than that.]

I went to the bridge after breakfast and stayed about 2 hours. I saw a couple of ships and fishing boats, but at one point I realized that what I thought were low-lying clouds to port were mountains. The coastal range at the tip of Africa. I even determined that I was looking at the Cape of Good Hope, dimly through heavy fog. The first sight of land since the Eastern Seaboard. After we changed course more eastward, I hoped we might be close enough to see more coastal mountaintops farther east.

I stared at the vague shapes of the Cape Mountains until mist and glare obscured them. It may have been my only chance to actually see Africa. Ever.

Lunch – grilled pork cutlet, roasted potatoes, green beans cooked with onion and loose sausage.

Went back up on the bridge for about an hour. Not much to be seen. We were about 20 miles south of the most southern bit of Africa, which has mountains, but it was too misty to see anything but a vague outline.

We were (at last) headed DUE EAST! Our southern journey was done. Later we would turn a bit more northeast, after we cleared Africa in a couple of days. Progress! I actually used my own binoculars (which are more powerful than the ones on the bridge) and took the GPS up to the bridge. It was good to see for myself our heading, speed and relation to the coast. On my GPS, it was less detailed and rougher than on the monitors on the bridge, of course, but good enough. The GPS map actually gave an idea of the terrain as far as hills, etc.

Supper – small lamb steak, boiled potatoes.

By my rough count it was 18 days without sight of land. Seemed like more. It looked like it would, once again, be too overcast to see the stars. I hoped we'd have one clear night on which to see them, especially the Southern Cross, before we got too far north. Having reached the Horn of Africa, it really did feel like I was on the way home. Technically we weren't yet halfway, distance or time-wise, but the fact that we were headed east, then northeast, which is the direction of Seattle, made it feel like we were homeward bound.

Email Home:

The World. Around it. On a ship. Mostly.

S34° 29.493' E17° 30.241'
Progress down Africa — Going around the sticky-downy bit at the southern tip.

We've finally got even with Capetown and will very soon - sometime today - be crossing from the Atlantic to the Indian Ocean at the Cape of Good Hope. It will be a bit bizarre to see something other than 120 as a heading. It's not light out yet (7:16 am - but it's winter here - shorter days) but later it will be interesting to see if there are any other ships visible. We'll be too far from shore to see any of South Africa, but it's interesting to know that we're so far south. Just about as far south as I was in Australia. It's been too overcast at night to see the Southern Cross, unfortunately, but I should have a few more opportunities. Yesterday I went outside on the bridge and the wind wasn't too strong. The weather was cool and pleasant. I understand you've been having some days in the 90s? I'll try to send you some of this Southern Hemisphere winter.

No other news - life on board goes on as usual. It's good to feel like I'm heading home. Long way

The World. Around it. On a ship. Mostly.

```
to go, but at least we're going in
the right direction!
```

The World. Around it. On a ship. Mostly.

Day 31 (26) 7/12/2016 Tuesday

S34° 39.261' E24° 47.298'

Speed 17kn Heading 80°

412 miles from yesterday's position. Av. Speed last 24 hr –18kn. 8857 miles from home.

Progress across Africa – 40 miles south of the southern coast about 100 miles e. of Port Elizabeth.

Our heading was ENE! It would get more N shortly, but how great not to be going SE anymore. I saw the Southern Cross last night. To accomplish this necessitated being outside at night, which was frowned upon by the Authorities. Rather than risk opening the heavy and noisy outer door, I climbed out my window to the porch outside and climbed back in head-first after star-gazing for a while. Fortunately the bed was just inside the window.

> [A few years ago, when in Australia, I remembered to look up one clear, dark night and I saw the Southern Cross shining brilliantly in an india-ink sky. It was one of the most beautiful things I'd ever seen. The view on this trip wasn't as dramatic, but I wonder how many Midwest Flatlanders like me have seen it even once, let alone twice.]

I went to the bridge in the morning to see if I could see any land around Port Elizabeth. We were still close to the coast, but it was too hazy. The sea was choppier, but the ride wasn't rough. When we were on the Atlantic, we seemed to be sailing against the waves and swells, but they seemed to be going in generally the same direction as us, in the Indian Ocean. No ships were to be seen.

Lunch – roast chicken, mashed potatoes.

Napped. We were rolling a bit more, side to side.

Supper - "Ox-tail stew." A couple of large ox-tails with a medium amount of meat stewed with potatoes, carrots and tomatoes. Not bad.

Email Home:
Don't have the numbers today, but we'll show up on the ship tracker site.
We're about 30 miles off the south coast of Africa, about 100 miles W. of Port Elizabeth. Seas remain surprisingly calm. A very smooth ride. I have a feeling it will be paid for at some point, with huge waves and gale-force winds, but so far, so good.
Yesterday I went up to the bridge in the morning and was looking north at some ships going by and realized that what I initially thought were some low-lying clouds was actually Africa! There is a coastal mountain range near Cape Town, and the tops of it were visible over the horizon. I was even able to make out where the Cape of Good Hope was. All shrouded in mist, of course, but now the fact remains that I have seen Africa. If we stay fairly close to the coast, I may see more today. Also, last night I noticed that it was at least partly clear, and I saw the Southern Cross. Not

The World. Around it. On a ship. Mostly.

bad for a Midwestern boy to now have seen it twice!
I hope all is well there. I miss you all and am saving up hugs for the babies. Paul will not seem at all like a baby when I'm back, I'm sure. He'll be a proper young gent. And Susie won't be a newborn. At least now I'm headed in their direction. We've turned left and are headed ENE!

The World. Around it. On a ship. Mostly.

Day 32 (27) 7/13/2016 Wednesday

S32° 54.353' E31° 45.420'

Speed 17kn Heading 80^0

417 miles from yesterday's position. Av. Speed last 24 hr –17kn. 9145 miles from home.

Progress across Africa – About 220 miles east of East London, South Africa.

We were definitely launched into the Indian Ocean. There was a long way to go yet, but we were into the next leg for sure. Smooth seas again. Also, again, the novelty of looking, while under sunny skies, and seeing, on the horizon, a mass of black clouds which tapered off side to side into fluffy white ones and, at the center, a clearly-defined column of rain falling from the darkest part of the clouds to the sea below.

Once again, when I looked at the wi-fi connection on the laptop, I saw another network. This time it's "Direct-rE-Bravia" "Bravia" sounds like a ship name. The connection was very weak, but I wondered if there was another ship close enough that I could momentarily see their WIFI? I should have checked when we were nearer Capetown and there were more ships. I made a note to remember to look again when we're near or in Port Kelang. What a hoot if I was able to get on line through another ship's network! Ivan said it most likely has to do with a game controller on board.

> [On the ship there was a WIFI network, to which my laptop had connected. I couldn't get the Internet with it, nor connect to the ship's email server. I never did find out what it was for.]

I got the schedule for the rest of the trip from Ivan. We were due get into Seattle in the evening of August 19th, to be able to disembark early on the 20th and get to the airport. I also got better idea of the time we were supposed to have in the ports. I made a note to email Nigel soon to see if we could get together in Hong Kong.

> [Nigel is a friend from other connections, who happens to live in Hong Kong.]

Ivan said – go to Kuala Lumpur, it's worth it. Also – "ten bucks" would buy a sim card for that location. I thought I might as well do it so as to keep in contact with the ship. I'll ask someone how that's done at some point.

Lunch – a bowl of beans with a couple of small ham slices and half a sausage in. Not too bad, but the beans needed to be cooked a bit longer.

Napped. Supper - baked fish (not bad) orange rice and roll-up wonton. They were out of lettuce, so no more green salad – just chopped-up tomatoes and carrots.

```
Email Home:
S32° 54.353' E31° 45.420'
Progress across Africa - 220 miles
east of East London, South Africa.
Now definitely started across the
Indian Ocean. We'll divert
slightly around Madagascar, but
it's almost a straight shot to the
north end of Sumatra, where we'll
head down the straights of
Mallacca. On the way, we'll pass
Reunion Island, just east of
Madagascar. I don't know why that
name sounds so familiar. I can't
google it, of course. I must have
read something about it at some
point.
```

The World. Around it. On a ship. Mostly.

I don't know yet if we're on the same schedule as far as ports that I anticipated. It's plausible that we'll reach Port Klang (or Kalang, or Kelang, depending on where you look) on the anticipated date, but it's too early to tell for sure. I was assured that the trip around Africa would take no longer than to go through the Suez, but I'm still having trouble believing it.

The sea looks pretty much the same, and the waves haven't been too rough, despite the early prediction of 5-meter waves about now. I've noticed that whereas the swell (direction of the ocean waves) was against us in the Atlantic, it seems to be going our way in the Indian, so far. Interesting. All due to winds, I'm told. All proceeds as normal - reading, napping, looking out at water. Thrills and chills at sea.

A request: could someone call and get Sam's email address? I've sent an email - some time ago - and haven't gotten a reply. He may be out of town, or just lazy, but I want to make sure I sent it to the right address. Thanks.

The World. Around it. On a ship. Mostly.

Day 33 (28) 7/14/2016 Thursday

S30° 27.302' E38° 43.476'

Speed 16kn Heading 62°

443 miles from yesterday's position. Av. Speed last 24 hr –19kn. 9483 miles from home.

Progress across Indian Ocean – Slightly east of Dar Es Salaam,Tanzania, Slightly South of Durban, S.A.

Got an email from Sam. Very nice. Sent an email to Nigel to see if he will be available in Hong Kong.

Did a half-hour on the treadmill while the steward made up the room. Later he came back with a tin of biscuits just like the one from before, and a smaller tin of butter cookies (shortbread). He must have looked into the first tin and seen that they were getting low. My guess was that I guessed right on how much to tip.

Sunny, and only a bit of choppiness. Some whitecaps. Smooth ride.

Lunch – "Leftover Soup" (My name for it – bits of other soups and suppers in it, plus pasta.) Pork stirfry. Ice cream bar. Napped wrote a bit in the new book. Not this one – another one.

Supper - 7 officers at a time in the dining room! All of the Europeans, I think. Supper was cubes of white meat chicken in a tomatoish sort of sauce. White rice. Big raised, iced doughnuts for dessert. I took one to my room. In the evening, I wrote a bit more in the new book. The other one.

```
Email Home:
S30° 27.302' E38° 43.476'
Progress   across   Indian  Ocean   –
Slightly    east    of    Dar    Es
Salaam,Tanzania,
Slightly South of Durban, SA
```

The World. Around it. On a ship. Mostly.

Hi to all - we've broken away from the coast of Africa and are south of the Mozambique channel. We're not going up the channel - we're heading straight for the north end of Sumatra. We're due for some more fairly dull days crossing the Indian Ocean. I got the proposed schedule for the rest of the trip yesterday. Most importantly, we'll be arriving in Seattle on the evening of August 19th. That means that I will be able to disembark fairly early on the 20th, and get myself straight to the airport. More discussion on that to follow, I'm sure.

It looks like there may (MAY) be time in Port Klang to get to Kuala Lumpur, about an hour and a half away. We'll see. Any suggestions as to what to do there on a very short visit will be welcome.

Also - one person on board has said that, while there, I should change the SIM card in my phone so as to be able to send and receive calls from the ship. My phone won't work over there as it is. He says it's easy to do and will cost very little. Have any of you ever done that? I've found the card in the back of my phone, but haven't tried to remove it. I

The World. Around it. On a ship. Mostly.

can't imagine that the whole process is as easy as all that. If it's that easy and cheap, however, I should do it. That person also expressed incredulity that, even though I wouldn't be able to make and receive phone calls with my phone as it is now, that I wouldn't be able to send and receive messages. Any thoughts? Messaging capability would eliminate the need for the sim card.

Plenty of time to try to get all of that worked out. I wish I'd brought the manual for the phone with me.

I got an email from Sam. Was that the result of someone calling him, or a coincidence?

The World. Around it. On a ship. Mostly.

Day 34 (29) 7/15/2016 Friday

S27° 54.729' E45° 20.572'

Speed 17kn Heading 65°

435 miles from yesterday's position. Av. Speed last 24 hr –18kn. 9732 miles from home.

Progress across Indian Ocean – 167 miles south of the southernmost point of Madagascar.

Last night I woke up in what I thought was the middle of the night with headache. I got up, took some aspirin, and, looking forward to more sleep, exited the bathroom. At this point the alarm went off. It was 6 AM. Bad words. Napped bigtime later. It was nice that I could see rest of trip on the Outlook calendar (in "Month View") all at once.

Just as I had been looking forward to breaking away from the Americas on the map, I was at this point looking forward to having Africa disappear off the left side of the screen and relating our position entirely to Asia. I was sure that in the final 10 days I'd want Asia to slide off to the left.

I was enjoying the trip and valuing it, but I was very ready to be home. There would be challenges to face, obligations to fulfill and decisions to make, but also grandkids and kids and others to see and hug. Home is good. "East, West, Home's Best." Is that Tolkien? In any case, I would be in a better position to testify to the truth of that statement than anybody I know.

Mid-morning. Sea had kicked up a bit – high winds. Not too much rock and roll at this point. Wrote some in the new book.

Lunch – beef vegetable soup in a sort of chicken stock. Boiled shrimp with heads on and meatballs. And fried rice. This time I shucked all of the shrimp at once and rinsed my fingers with a little vinegar and then water to keep down the shrimp smell. It seemed to work.

Got emails from Alice re: Kuala Lumpur – would need time to study them. As I was at email computer, the second officer told me we're expecting some rough seas in the next couple of days – "lots of rolling" and that I should not go on deck. Around the "accommodation" it would be OK to go outside, but not on deck. It would be interesting to see how rough it would get and how well I would react.

Napped. Saw one of the new container ships with the accommodation and bridge near the bow and the stack still near the stern.

Looked out of the window – something I noticed – how empty the sky was of airplanes. Living fairly near to two airports, I'm used to seeing planes most of the time, during the day. Out there, nothing. Odd.

Supper – pizza. Ham and pepperoni, but also mushroom, green pepper, onion and olive. Not bad, actually.

```
Email Home:
S27° 54.729' E45° 20.572'
Progress across Indian Ocean - 167
miles  south  of  the  southernmost
point of Madagascar.
Slowly  but  surely  pulling  away
from  Africa,  seeing  it  slide
farther to left on the map on the
computer,  just  as  I  saw  South
America  slide  left  a  couple  of
weeks ago.  Soon the map will be
all Asia. Progress!
If  anyone  has  suggestions  as  to
what  to  do  and  see  in  Kuala
```

The World. Around it. On a ship. Mostly.

Lumpur, let me know. Remember, I can't google from here. And yes, I should have done all of that before leaving, but I was figuring that there wouldn't be time to get there. Also - any thoughts on the phone/sim card matter will be welcome.

No news, really. The rough seas promised for the rounding of the Horn never materialized, thankfully. What we'll run into in the Indian Ocean and the Pacific remains to be seen. I guess that we can still look forward to some bad weather in Asia this time of year.

The World. Around it. On a ship. Mostly.

Day 35 (30) 7/16/2016 Saturday

S25° 26.184' E51° 37.498'

Speed 16kn Heading 68°

423 miles from yesterday's position. Av. Speed last 24 hr –17kn. 9944 miles from home.

Progress across Indian Ocean – Due East of Pretoria SA, Due south of northeast point of Somalia.

Rocking a bit more. I wondered how rough it would get. I was actually farther from home at that point than when in I was in Australia, "as the crow flies". I looked through the work I'd done on the new book. Not bad, but it will need smoothing as scenes are assembled. I'm up to 30 pages and just now introduced the main plot driver. Time to do laundry.

The Sun was out – still rough water – many whitecaps – rainbows in the spindrift. I discovered that, as lovely as they are, the little rainbows that sometimes form in the mist coming off the waves are nearly impossible (for me) to photograph. Presumably the winds are still strong. 30 min on treadmill while the steward made up the room.

Officers I met on the elevator said it will get rougher, and that could affect the date we get into port. Made a note to keep track of that.

The steward left full packages of Ritz and saltine crackers in my cabin.

Lunch – bean and ham soup. Again, the beans were not done enough. Grilled chicken "cutlet." Potato salad.

Napped. I seemed to have lost my pocket comb. It was not in the laundry or anyplace else.

The World. Around it. On a ship. Mostly.

[This trivial incident, the loss of my pocket comb, was a watershed occurrence for several concepts. Stay tuned and remember that it happened on Day 35, just over halfway through the journey.]

An officer on bridge said that we could expect a storm "Maybe tomorrow." We seemed to have slowed down a bit, maybe to let the storm dissipate or move before we get to it. The Captain said that this is S.O.P.

Supper – pork and liver stew. Not a favorite.

Email Home:
S25° 26.184' E51° 37.498'
Progress across Indian Ocean – Due East of Pretoria SA, Due south of northeast point of Somalia
We've just about gotten away from Africa as a reference point - soon to be in Mid-Indian Ocean. I noticed that, As The Crow Flies, I'm actually farther from home here than I was when in Australia. That won't last long, though. In just a few days, we'll reach the halfway point (ATCF) and the distance from home will start getting smaller rather than larger, which it's still doing.
Alice - I've studied the info you sent and it sounds like a good itinerary. Ed mentioned some of the same places. I'll check with the Port Agent as to the best way to get to and from KL. I've spotted the Port Kelang train

The World. Around it. On a ship. Mostly.

station on the map of Port Kelang (or Kalang) I printed out. From what people on board say, the Port Agent is likely to be helpful, and "everybody" takes American Dollars. I remain somewhat skeptical, but we'll see. I expect that it would be somewhat interesting just to hang around Port Kelang for a while, if I can't get into KL.

We're into some rougher water today, but so far nothing too bad. Last night's supper was pizza - Pepperoni and Ham! It had other things on it like green pepper, mushroom and olives, but wasn't bad at all. Not like Connie's, but not bad.

The World. Around it. On a ship. Mostly.

Day 36 (31) 7/17/2016 Sunday

S23° 03.429' E57° 32.270'

Speed 15kn Heading 68°

407 miles from yesterday's position. Av. Speed last 24 hr –17kn. 10146 miles from home.

Progress across Indian Ocean – 166 miles SW of Reunion Island.

Sea – not too rough. Rolled a bit more than previous. I wondered if we'll get the expected rough seas soon? Looked like maybe storms on the horizon on starboard side, out my window. I would go to bridge when there was more light. On the bridge, Ivan said there will probably be a storm that night.

Lunch – small steak, overdone fries, corn. Tripe soup, which must be a big favorite with the crew. The broth is good, though.

Napped. At 3:00 – still not too rough. Rolling more than usual.

Supper – spaghetti with the usual white mushroom sauce, this time with a little ham in. I went to the bridge after supper – they said that the next couple of days should be about like this – meaning choppy seas and moderate rolling. One guy (the Second Officer?) said that the ship was built so that it would never move to the point that things fall off shelves. Good to hear it.

> **Email Home:**
> S23° 03.429' E57° 32.270'
> Progress across Indian Ocean - 166 miles SW of Reunion Island.
> Now for another week or so of 360-degree horizons. It will take 7 days or so, depending on weather, to get to the north end of the Straits of Mellacca. At that point, and for some time after, we

should show up on the ship-tracking site. The guys on the bridge said yesterday that the big storm we're expecting should come "Maybe tomorrow," so I'm considering battening down the hatches and taking a preventive Dramamine. I've been promised rough seas, and so far just a bit of "rock and roll".

I must see if there is any information on board on our destinations. They don't have a rack of tourist brochures, but maybe they have a map or some such.

At this point, I am over 10,000 miles from home, As The Crow Flies. That's a lot of miles. Soon, however, as I may have said, the distance home will start getting smaller rather than larger. Looking forward to that.

The World. Around it. On a ship. Mostly.

Day 37 (32) 7/18/2016 Monday

S20° 40.575' E63° 21.532'

Speed 16 kn Heading 68^0

403 miles from yesterday's position. Av. Speed last 24 hr –16kn. 10387 miles from home.

Progress across Indian Ocean – 502 miles E of Reunion Island

Finally I could arrange the Basecamp map so as to see none of Africa - only Asia (with a bit of the Mideast). A milestone of sorts. Still pretty choppy – high winds – rolling a fair amount.

On bridge, I talked with the Captain about going ashore. He gave me more lessons on the ship's course and avoiding tropical depressions – which he did south of Madagascar. Apparently there had been a Tropical Depression near Madagascar as we rounded the south end of Africa. It had started going "Cyclonic" (spinning) and kicking up very large waves, so he altered our course somewhat south to avoid all of that. It didn't look like much of a deviation on the map, but it would cause us to have to put on some speed in order to try to stay on schedule. He took me down to the office to show me displays on his personal PC.

Looked like – from his computer map prediction – that it would get smoother little by little till we got to the top end of Sumatra where it would be pretty calm. I think that he said that recently – in the last couple of days – we were within 1 meter of wave height of being outside the recommended range for this ship. Not terribly dangerous but it was interesting to reflect on how the ship performed as regarded steadiness in that time. There was no feeling of danger, or even that anything might be amiss. So under normal circumstances the ride should not ever get much rougher than it had been over the last couple of days.

He said he'll have someone make me a list of DVDs which were available.

Lunch – grilled pork cutlet, mashed potatoes, cabbage. Borscht.

I skipped my afternoon nap but managed to fall asleep reading. So much for skipping my nap.

Supper – fried breaded fish filet. Orange rice. Rolled-up wonton.

```
Email Home:
S20° 40.575' E63° 21.532'
Progress across Indian Ocean - 502
miles W of Reunion Island
Still roughish sea and a good deal
of rolling.  Yesterday I went to
the bridge and one of the officers
explained how, even in very rough
seas, this ship is designed not to
bounce around to the point that
things fall off shelves. Very glad
to hear it.
As far as I can tell, we should be
having these conditions for the
next couple of days.
Nothing much new - same sort of
routine.  It's interesting to know
where we are, from looking at the
map, but the view has been just
about the same since we left
Charleston.      Obviously    the
condition of the sea changes, and
the   clouds   and   rain   pattern
changes, but it's mostly horizon
surrounding us and us floating
```

The World. Around it. On a ship. Mostly.

along in our 30-or-so-mile-in-diameter circle.
Sometimes we see a passing ship. In a few days, however, we'll have more company and will start to see land, then we will be at Port Kelang. For a while after that, the trip will be more broken up by port stops and be less monotonous. Still, it's cool to know that we're in the middle (almost) of the Indian Ocean with India to the north, even if I can't see it.

The World. Around it. On a ship. Mostly.

Day 38 (33) 7/19/2016 Tuesday

S17° 15.999' E68° 30.104'

Speed 15 kn Heading 46⁰

408 miles from yesterday's position. Av. Speed last 24 hr –17kn. 10369 miles from home.

(P.S. added on 7-20. I believed that this would be the farthest distance from home I would see.)

Progress across Indian Ocean – Straight south of Kabul, Pakistan; Straight west of southernmost point of Gulf of Carpentaria, Australia.

I was starting to dream of food. Not that the food on board was bad, it was just very much the same, and there was no choice. No decision to have a certain kind of food and then going out and getting it. Hopefully I'd get some sort of break from that in Kuala Lumpur. Maybe a miracle will happen and I'd find a Portillo's. Or a branch of El Burrito Loco.

I was starting to see some light in the sky before breakfast, from getting farther north. I could wrangle the map to see the rest of trip up through the Tsuraru Straight between Honshu and Hokkaido, Japan. From there it would be straight across the Pacific to Seattle.

30 min on treadmill while the steward made up the room. The next day would be the halfway point of the number (68) of days at sea. The previous Saturday had been the halfway point between getting on the plane at O'Hare and flying back to Chicago from Seattle.

Lunch – grilled chicken cutlet, roast potatoes.

The Chief Engineer said that the roughness and rock and roll we'd had was about as bad as it gets on this ship. He was a bit surprised I hadn't (knock wood) been sick. Just that one (knock wood) vertigo session and the morning of feeling generally weird. No nausea. And those were both before the rough weather. Getting sunny – sea still choppy. Napped.

Fire alarm! I thought that the Captain had said, in the follow-up announcement: "This is real. This is real. This is real." I went to the bridge and was told that it was "Just a procedure". Then I realized what he had said was: "Dees ees dreel. Dees ees dreel. Dees ees dreel."   The Captain stressed that there would be an inspector on board between Port Kelang and Vung Tau and that it was vital that, in case of alarms and drills, of which there might be several, I should go to the bridge without fail to prove that they have trained me correctly.

Email Home:
S17° 15.999' E68° 30.104'
Progress across Indian Ocean – Straight south of Kabul, Pakistan; Straight west (and this time I really mean west) of southernmost point of Gulf of Carpentaria, Australia
Storms abating somewhat. Apparently what we went through had been upgraded from a "Tropical Depression" (which sounds like when you're sitting on the beach and you look out and the sea just isn't blue enough and the sand isn't yellow enough and the waiter isn't bringing your mai-tai fast enough) to a "cyclone" which merely means, I'm told, that the air around the center has started to rotate.

The World. Around it. On a ship. Mostly.

There's some light in the sky before breakfast (which happens at 7AM) these past couple of mornings, indicating we're getting farther north. Hopefully we'll have clear sailing between here and our first port, (Port Kelang, which I seem to spell differently every time I type it.)

I've started to dream of food. Do you suppose Portillo's has a branch in KL? (Don't laugh - there are Portillo's clones in Japan) or maybe El Burrito Loco has a place there? You can tell this is a British email program. Spell-check wanted me to spell "center" "centre" and it doesn't know the word "burrito".

Doing well - nothing but sea to see. (What was that old musical that had the song - "We joined the Navy to see the world but what did we see? We saw the sea."?)

The World. Around it. On a ship. Mostly.

Day 39 (34) 7/20/2016 Wednesday

S13° 29.119' E73° 06.088'

Speed 15 kn Heading 46°

401 miles from yesterday's position. Av. Speed last 24 hr –17kn. 10300 miles from home.

Progress across Indian Ocean – Straight south of Surat, India; Straight west of middle of the right-hand sticky-uppy bit of Australia.

We were smack-dab in the middle of the Indian Ocean. In terms of the original estimate of 68 days at sea – which seemed plausible at this point – halfway! The halfway point between when I got on the plane to go to Newark Airport and when I'll fly home (according to plan) was the previous Saturday. I made a note to look at it more carefully, but it looked like the point when I was getting closer to home rather than farther away happened a couple of days before, earlier than I thought. Checked it out after breakfast.

Actually, at a rough estimate, using "Measure" in Basecamp, it looked like the distance to home started getting smaller today, and would continue to do so for the rest of the trip. I had assumed that it would happen when the line on the map used for measuring distances flipped over from measuring west-east to east-west, but it seemed to be happening sooner. I looked again – using "Measure" – and it looked kosher. Made a note to keep track as days go by. The distance yesterday – which may have been the longest distance – was 10369 miles from home.

I worked on the new book a bit.

Lunch – lentil soup, quite good, large pieces of pork. Whole roasted chicken breast. Large, a bit dry. Mashed potatoes, just warm enough to melt soft butter. And on the plate, where you would expect a vegetable – green beans, broccoli – was a small pile of cut-up bits of ham. Presented just as if they were vegetable. So not only do the vegetables contain meat, in this case the vegetables ARE meat. To be fair, it probably has to do with the fact that the last time we took on food supplies was 34 days previously. For example, the fresh salad veg - lettuce, tomatoes, were gone. The mashed potatoes were probably from a box. The longer-lasting vegetables – onions and potatoes for example, were still in evidence. It would be interesting to see what would happen after Kuala Lumpur.

Napped. Had bit of migraine so took pills and napped some more.

Supper – pork chunks on skewer with tomatoes and onions. Rice pilaf. Pork was underdone, so I nuked it 3 minutes.

Asked captain about list of DVDs and he said "You haff not receefed?" and picked up the phone. I haff a feeling that somebody receefed a tongue-lashing in an Eastern European language. I wondered when the list will arrive?

About a half-hour later, at my room, one of the crew arrived with the list and said that he would be back in a half hour. He was. I wondered when the DVDs would arrive? Of maybe a hundred on the list, I recognized only about a dozen titles. It would be interesting to see what the ones I selected by title are like. It would be a break from Dr. Who, although I didn't really need one. The kid never showed with DVDs. Maybe the next day.

Email Home:
```
S13° 29.119' E73° 06.088'
Progress across Indian Ocean -
Straight south of Surat, India;
Straight west of middle of the
right-hand sticky-uppy bit of
Australia.
```

The World. Around it. On a ship. Mostly.

Sticky-uppy bit? Guess who's been reading P.G. Wodehouse. Weather better - some sun yesterday. Still a fair amount of "rock and roll" but nothing disturbing. Very much looking forward to going ashore in a few days, hopefully to Kuala Lumpur. Alice - you mentioned a train that goes from Port Kelang to KL. I believe that I have spotted the Port Kelang station on a map I printed out. Do you have any other data on that train? Does it run all night? Etc?

Here's a question that's not time-sensitive but has been on my mind - every couple of days, we turn our clocks and such ahead one hour for the time zones. The announcement comes: "1700 hours will become 1800 hours." The ship's clocks all automatically move forward, and I change my watch, kindle, phone and computer. We will be crossing the International Date Line at some point on the Pacific, say August 15th or so. Will they be saying: "1700 hours will become 1800 hours August 16th?" I'm a bit shaky on that concept. I get the general idea and am not superstitious enough to believe that I will have

The World. Around it. On a ship. Mostly.

lost (or gained, if I've got that wrong) a day in my life. (I still remember Grandma and her references to being on "Fast Time.") Can anybody clear that up for me? As you know, I can't google it for myself, so I depend on you all. I'd be embarrassed to ask the officers on the ship, but you all already know that there are things about the world that baffle me.

The World. Around it. On a ship. Mostly.

Day 40 (35) 7/21/2016 Thursday

S9° 45.546' E77° 24.937'

Speed 16 kn Heading 65°

389 miles from yesterday's position. Av. Speed last 24 hr –16kn. 10188 miles from home.

Progress across Indian Ocean – Straight south of Coimbatore, India; Straight west of slightly north of the southern tip of Sumba Island.

Rain and Rock and Roll. The sea was still quite choppy – I guessed waves of 3-4 meters from what the captain had said the other day. So far so good re: seasickness. No nausea. It looked like the miles from home had topped out. At a couple of points around China they would bump up a bit due to following the coast, but would never go back over 10369, the highest number from Tuesday.

Nothing to do but wait for the DVDs. Just like being at home, waiting at home for UPS.

I went on the treadmill while the steward made up the room. Got back – 1 DVD copy sitting on the counter, with a note – "Please try this one." I put it in the laptop and it played just fine. I went down to the recreation room and hooked up the DVD player in there, but it didn't work. The tray wouldn't operate. That's OK – I'd probably watch on my laptop anyway. The DVD was a sci-fi, with dialog in, I think, Spanish, and subtitles in, I think, Klingon. I thought that there might not have been much point in asking for any but American titles – or British – they might have, in fact, been dubbed into something else. And I wasn't sure I'd know for sure which ones they are. We'd see. Maybe there were some Chaplin or Keaton films? Didn't see any.

Lunch – chicken soup and "Beef Fatties" according to the menu card. They came with slaw and overdone, cold fries. No sign of the kid with the DVDs. Later he brought a DVD with three movies on it – arty European stuff with Gallifreyan subtitles (I think).

Supper – since the clock moved forward again – 1700 became 1800 – I wasn't very hungry and also knew that the main course was calamari, fried. Not a big favorite. Just had soup. Good chicken soup in fact.

Email Home:
S9° 45.546' E77° 24.937'
Progress across Indian Ocean – Straight south of Coimbatore, India;
Straight west of slightly north of the southern tip of Sumba Island.
I seem to be turning these updates into a sort of Geography Quiz, making you get out the Atlas and see where, for example, Sumba Island is. (Hint - take a left - or maybe right - at East Timor.)
Still pitching and rolling pretty good. Pitching is when we rock fore to aft, and rolling is when we rock port to starboard. I was in the exercise room the other day. There's a ping-pong table there and one of the balls had fallen to the floor. It was rolling all over from the motion of the ship, and sometimes it described a near-perfect circle, as the pitching and rolling evened out. Sometimes as the bow goes down, a large wave (or swell) will

The World. Around it. On a ship. Mostly.

hit the bow at just the right moment and angle and a shudder goes all through the whole ship. I'm told that this is called "The Hammer" and is harmless. I've never figured that being hit by a hammer would be harmless, but so far so good.

The captain had a crewman bring to my cabin a list of DVDs available. I looked at the list of maybe a hundred titles and recognized only about a dozen. The rest are probably European, maybe, in fact, Rumanian. Or French. I checked off a few almost at random. It will be interesting to see what I get. I'm not worried if some turn out to be questionable. I'll never see these people again. So now I have to wait in my cabin for him to bring the DVDs. In the middle of the Indian Ocean, and I'm waiting at home for a delivery! Might as well be home waiting for UPS!

The World. Around it. On a ship. Mostly.

Day 41 (36) 7/22/2016 Friday

S5° 49.308' E81° 48.201'

Speed 16 kn Heading 50^0

405 miles from yesterday's position. Av. Speed last 24 hr –16kn. 10032 miles from home.

Progress across Indian Ocean – Straight south of Vijayawada, India; Straight west of the southern tip of Sumatra.

OK – it must be said – over the next couple of days I would probably be the closest to Java (just over 1000 miles) that I would ever be while drinking coffee. (Java – get it?) Sorry. Miles from home decreasing! Also – on Sunday we would be, longitudinally speaking, halfway around the world.

A joke written after looking at the map of the South Pacific:

> "....A couple of hundred years ago, in the south Pacific, you would hear conversations like this:
>
>> "Hi! I just arrived on your island! Paddled all the way from my island and I'm really hungry. Got any fish?"
>>
>> "What are you, crazy? That's all we got - fish. Fish and fruit. Here - have a halibut and a mango."
>>
>> "Thanks! I'm from the Marshall Islands - what are these islands called?"
>>
>> "No idea. No white guy has showed up to name them yet...."
>
> Of course, after a while the islands all had names. Nice names: Cook Islands, Marshall Islands, Solomon Islands, Christmas Island. Everybody got

The World. Around it. On a ship. Mostly.

along.... Of course, the Solomon Islands couldn't join the Country Club...."

Overcast – rain – sea somewhat less rough.

I asked Ivan for his recommendations of places to go, things to see in Kuala Lumpur.

Lunch – bean stew with ham and sausage. I felt like needlepointing a sampler for the cook to hang in his kitchen saying "Soak Beans Overnight." They're not supposed to be crunchy when served.

Still raining. On the bridge, it was so foggy we couldn't see much past the navigation lights at the bow. Even though raining, deck crew was using a pressure-cleaner on the exterior of the "Accommodation."

Napped. The First Officer – who was apparently in charge of young man that brings videos - said they will supply them on a thumb drive since I was watching on my laptop.

Supper – chunks of whitemeat chicken in a tomato sauce. The sauce was a bit olive-intensive, but not bad. Potato pancakes. Wine – the Third Officer finally coughed up another bottle. The steward sat and chatted – not easy considering I understand about his every 3rd or 4th word, but we did ok. He mentioned another passenger would be getting on in Hong Kong and asked me if I had heard anything about nationality of new passenger, etc. I hadn't. No sign of more videos.

Email Home:
```
S5° 49.308' E81° 48.201'
Progress   across   Indian   Ocean   –
Straight   south   of   Vijayawada,
India;   Straight   west   of   the
southern tip of Sumatra.
```

The World. Around it. On a ship. Mostly.

In a couple of days we'll be at the northern tip of Sumatra, and from then on until we depart Korea, we'll once again be mostly coastal. Won't hug the shore the whole time, but we'll bounce off of the east coast of Asia several times. At some point soon, we will be, East-to-West-wise, halfway around the world. Weather is calming down a bit, the ride is getting smoother, no news to speak of.

The World. Around it. On a ship. Mostly.

Day 42 (37) 7/23/2016 Saturday

S1° 29.016' E86° 31.951'

Speed 15 kn Heading 45^0

439 miles from yesterday's position. Av. Speed last 24 hr –18kn. 9772 miles from home.

Progress across Indian Ocean – Straight south of Dhanbad, India; Straight west of a point about ¾ down the island of Pulau Siberut.

I looked out the window before dawn and saw the lights, bow and stern, of another ship not too distant. Somehow it was very cool.

I had trouble sleeping the previous night. The trip seemed to be sending me a bit round the bend. At one point I woke up from a dream in which something grabbed me suddenly, and I woke flailing my arms and I may have shrieked a bit. Later I woke up chuckling because I'd told myself something funny. The thing was – calling someone a "Copsupper."

A dream image – I had a hunk of shiny black plastic about the size and shape of a shoebox. With a sharp bread knife, I cut a thin slice off the end. It's a Kindle. Slice a bit thinner, it's an iPad.

There was a general oil/exhaust smell in the room last night as if the AC intake was sucking up fumes from the smokestack. May have had something to do with the bad night's sleep and the dreams?

I also dreamed up a title for this book when I write up these notes:

The World.

Around it.

On a Ship.

Mostly.

The World. Around it. On a ship. Mostly.

Overcast and some rain. Sea choppy but not as rough. Ride smoother, but still some R&R.

I went up to the bridge. There seemed to be more ship traffic than previously – going to and from Kelang and Singapore, I suppose.

Lunch – grilled pork cutlet, warmish mashed potatoes, cabbage.

Started laundry – I wanted to do it earlier, but one of the washers didn't seem to be working, and the other one was in use. The wash/rinse/spin cycle, at the setting I use, is 189 minutes. About 5 times longer than at home. Frontloaders take longer, I guess. Then there's drying – usually over 2 hours.

Napped. After nap – 5:00 or so – we crossed the equator again, and were back in the Northern Hemisphere. And I was going to compare the ways the water drained from the sink on either side of the Equator. Maybe I can ask the captain to go back a few miles. Ya think?

Supper – pizza – pepperoni and ham – actually better than last time. Laundry finally got done.

```
Email Home:
S1° 29.016' E86° 31.951'
Progress across Indian Ocean -
Straight south of Dhanbad India;
Straight west of a point about ¾
down the island of Pulau Siberut
Monday morning we should be at the
northern tip of Sumatra. I hope
the weather is better at that
point - it's been raining quite a
bit lately. Hoping for sunny skies
when I try to get to KL.
Once we start hitting the coastal
cities, these dispatches may not
```

The World. Around it. On a ship. Mostly.

be as regular, but as far as ship position, the tracking site should have us in view for the following week at least, in fact, until we start east across the pacific.

The other day the Captain gave me a quick rundown on the ports, most of which I remember. Some sound like they will be worth visiting, some don't. I realized yesterday that for a few days it will be fairly easy to guess about what time it is there, because we will be straight through the globe from Central Time, so, as it's 7:30 am here, it's 7:30 pm there, if I've got that right.

Looking forward as always to news from home, hoping you are all doing OK. Any further thoughts on KL will be appreciated.

The World. Around it. On a ship. Mostly.

Day 43 (38) 7/24/2016 Sunday

N3° 01.016' E91° 23.835'

Speed 17 kn Heading 46°

456 miles from yesterday's position. Av. Speed last 24 hr –19kn. 9500 miles from home.

Progress across Indian Ocean – Straight south of Dhaka, Bangladesh; Straight west of Port Kelang, Malaysia (but we've got to go around the north end of Sumatra to get there.)

The sea was much calmer, still with a bit of chop. The ride was smoother, but with a fair amount of gentle rolling. This was caused by the swell, although it was no more than one meter, hitting us at an angle at the stern.

Mostly cloudy, no rain. Went to the bridge. We were running at 80 rpm (normal is 60) and going therefore about 20kn (23.0156 MPH) rather than 16. "To clean the supercharger – diesel", according to the Captain. I talked to Ivan and the Captain about Kuala Lumpur. I'd need to be in the ship's office on the Upper Deck at 7:00 AM Tuesday to talk to the port agent and do passport things. Hopefully also to get info re: transport, etc. as well.

Interesting. I was talking with Ivan, the Third Officer. (He was alone on the bridge.) The First Officer came on, and Ivan was less inclined to chat, but not stiff. The Captain came on the bridge, and Ivan practically snapped to attention, and stopped chatting. I picked up on that right away, I'm proud to say.

A couple of days before, the First Officer had said something about getting me movies on a thumb drive, but so far nothing. I wondered if I had to bring them my thumb drive? Nobody had said so. I will ask at some point, but didn't want to seem to nag especially about something as trivial as movies.

The World. Around it. On a ship. Mostly.

Lunch – small steak with overdone, cool fries and corn. The Steward said something that sounded like "2 more week" and I realized from his following words, gestures and expression that the present cook would be leaving in two weeks and that the steward thought that would be a very good thing. To have a different cook for the last couple weeks of the trip had about a 50-50 chance of being an improvement, but the steward seems to think that it will be better than it is now, at least. We would see. Napped.

Supper was a "Hot Dog". A fluffy bun with a sausage on it about the general size and shape of a hot dog, wrapped in a slice of bacon and covered with shredded cheese, with a slathering of hidden mayonnaise underneath. I asked for mustard and the steward brought Dijon. I scraped off the mayo and put on mustard. It was just this side of edible. On the side, chow mein noodles.

Mystery – at this meal, the bottle of ketchup was missing from the table. They must have known that, being from Chicago, I would have been mortally offended to see ketchup at that meal, being hot dogs and me being from Chicago. Oddly, the only other meal when the ketchup was missing was the night we had "Burger." That was one of the very few meals when I would have wanted it. Mystery upon mystery.

We'd be at the tip of Sumatra midnight-ish. Before turning in I'd have to see if I can see any lights. The First Officer said that the apprentice would come to see me and pick up a thumb drive from me to put movies on. When? Who knows? Heard from Nigel and we may be able to get together in Hong Kong.

Email Home:
N3° 01.016' E91° 23.835'
Progress across Indian Ocean – Straight south of Dhaka, Bangladesh;

The World. Around it. On a ship. Mostly.

Straight west of Port Kelang, Malaysia (but we've got to go around the
north end of Sumatra to get there.)

Back in the Northern Hemisphere! Crossed the equator yesterday. And I was going to compare how the water drains from the sink (clockwise vs counterclockwise) and missed my chance. Oh, well.
The sea is much smoother, and the rocking is much gentler. It's been interesting to walk across my room and start off uphill and end up downhill. I expect that in the Straits of Mellacca, which we will enter early tomorrow morning, the water will be relatively even. The Indian Ocean threw some weather at us - nothing like a full-fledged Typhoon or such - but "cyclonic" winds and rain. Not to mention 5-meter waves or higher. The China Sea and the Pacific Ocean will have their chances soon, but we've weathered so far.
Tomorrow I'll prep for KL. Alice, if you have any further thoughts on that, I will be glad to have them. I'll be printing out the itinerary you sent. We should get

The World. Around it. On a ship. Mostly.

there early Tuesday and have Tuesday in port.
Adventure Time!

The World. Around it. On a ship. Mostly.

Day 44 (39) 7/25/2016 Monday

N5° 54.048' E96° 30.531'

Speed 15 kn Heading 100^0

404 (ATCF) miles from yesterday's position. Av. Speed last 24 hr –18kn. 9346 miles from home.

Progress down Strait of Malacca – 32 miles north of the center of the top of Sumatra.

Sea calm, ride very smooth.

I looked out at about midnight and saw some ship lights and a glow of shore lights, and two flashing lights – lighthouses?

> [To see other ships and shore lights and features was, at that point, a big deal. We had been at sea 39 days, most of the time in isolation within our 30-mile-diameter bubble]

We were passing just north of northern tip of Sumatra. After breakfast I looked out and saw 2 container ships and one tanker nearby and another ship in the distance. Lots of company – and that was just on the starboard side! When I first looked around, it was not fully light and was a bit foggy – no shoreline was visible, but it was probably over the horizon anyway. The strait was fairly wide there. Base camp showed that the closest shore – Sumatra – was about 39 miles away. It wouldn't have been visible even if the weather had been clear.

I saw an Asian-looking fishing boat in the distance. It was now sunny, and the boat was a brilliant blue (seemingly the favorite color for fishing boats in some parts of Asia) with accents of bright red and gold. It looked to be made of wood. It had a small "wheelhouse" on the superstructure, and had the high, pointed bow that seemed to characterize just about every fishing boat I saw. The deck was covered with unidentifiable gear, and poles and shafts with complicated systems of lines and pulleys stuck up higher than

The World. Around it. On a ship. Mostly.

the superstructure. There were objects in water – logs, trash. We weren't in the middle of the ocean any more.

I went up to the bridge – Ivan said "You just missed – 5 minutes – 3 whales!" I actually saw some in the far distance to stern a bit later. I saw another fishing boat, Sumatran mountains above the horizon, in clouds, (like Africa, the only glimpse I was to have of Sumatra was a dark outline of mountaintops just on the horizon) and several more ships.

The Captain explained some things, like the fact that we were about 150 ft. above the water. I had wondered about that. Officers and crew on the bridge were scanning the water ahead of us with binoculars. I guessed that they were looking for small boats that wouldn't show up on radar, so we didn't just run right over them. I felt the atmosphere on the bridge starting to seem like I shouldn't be there. As I left, Ivan gave me a very stern look. No idea why.

Lunch – beef vegetable soup – with beans – and the beans weren't crunchy! Pork and liver stew, and I managed to avoid most of the liver this time.

Napped. Got up from nap, looked outside my window – brilliant sunshine and a very decorative fishing boat, much like the one this morning, right outside.

I took my folding chair, a water bottle, the Garmin, my binoculars and my camera to the porch on the starboard side, just outside my window. I was in the shade with a nice breeze, there were ships and boats in the sun and it was all very pleasant. Some of the boats seemed to be crabbers, tying up at floats. I saw one boat with a net out. At times, there was a lot of trash in the water. The worst offender – plastic bottles.

Supper – 2 lamb chops, cold roast potatoes. The only bread left was hamburger buns, stale. Dessert – rolled-up "pancake" (a leathery crepe-like thing, served room temperature) spread with

Nutella. Not as good as it sounds. And it doesn't sound that good, does it?

I was getting conflicting info re: the next day and our port time in Port Kelang, near Kuala Lumpur. On the bridge earlier the Captain talked about getting that day at 1700 (5:00 PM). A few minutes later I asked about that and he showed me the printed schedule with arrival at 7:00 AM the next day. At supper, the Chief Engineer told me about the 1700 arrival, then anchoring until an undetermined time.

I went to the bridge to see if there was any fresh any info posted, and the Second Officer said that we will get "alongside" at 7:00 AM the next morning. I didn't know what to think, so I kept my eyes and ears open. Any Kuala Lumpur plans were in danger of getting seriously messed up. It occurred to me that, at time of writing, it was after 1600 hours. Would we arrive in less than an hour? According to the Garmin and Basecamp, we were 190 miles from Port Kelang. Our current speed was about 12 kn. That made it about 15 hours to Port Kelang. That would put us there at 10:00 AM the next day. WTF?

I shortly thereafter saw on a whiteboard near the elevator on U Deck: "Arrival Delay." Maybe we'd anchor outside the port and go into port at 1700 tomorrow? And leave when? I guessed that the atmosphere on the bridge earlier was about the delay. I remember Ivan picking up the phone and after listening a bit, he made a disgusted noise. That was probably when he was informed of the delay. He was to leave the ship in Port Kelang. So what of the big day in KL? Who knew?

```
Email Home:
N5° 54.048' E96° 30.531'
Progress down Strait of Malacca -
43 miles north of the center of
the top of Sumatra.
```

The World. Around it. On a ship. Mostly.

We are entering the Strait of Melacca. Last night about midnight I looked out of the window and saw, beside the lights of a couple other ships, a glow on the horizon indicating land, and the blinking of a couple of distant lighthouses. We were passing the islands that are just off the northern tip of Sumatra. Now we are just north of Sumatra, and starting down the strait.

Depending on our route, there may not be much to see. If we stay close to the coast (either side) I will perhaps be able to see the coastline, but if we stay in the middle, especially here in the wider northern end of the strait, it will be too wide to see anything but water. On a good day, from the bridge, the horizon is about 15 miles away, making a circle 30 miles in diameter with us in the middle, so anything over 15 miles away is over the horizon. Except maybe a mountain. It might stick up high enough to see the top, through binoculars.

Tomorrow, with luck, Kuala Lumpur. I may not be sending a dispatch tomorrow morning, but will send info asap re: the shore excursion. I heard from my friend in Hong

Kong and we may be able to get together there briefly. That will be nice.

So - the Great Adventure continues. As soon as it gets lighter, I'll go to the bridge to see what I can see. A lot of the day will be spent checking and double-checking that I'm ready for tomorrow.

The World. Around it. On a ship. Mostly.

Day 45 (40) 7/26/2016 Tuesday

N2° 59.166' E100° 48.314'

Speed 10 kn Heading 125°

357 miles from yesterday's position. Av. Speed last 24 hr –14kn. 9512 miles from home.

Approaching Port Kelang (6:20 am). 36 miles due west.

So – 10:00 AM. The captain just did a fancy and excruciatingly slow job of diagonal parking outside the port. We were at anchor with many other ships outside of Port Kelang, waiting for a pilot, probably until late in the afternoon. There was a possibility of getting a berth that evening. What that meant in regard to getting on shore was unknown at that point. It was interesting that, though we were at anchor in a very calm harbor, and the ship was moving very little, I still felt the motion, like what happens when one goes ashore – or so I'm told.

Lunch - Soup - vegetable with cut-up pork ribs with a fair amount of meat on - not bad - and grilled whitemeat chicken, mashed potatoes and some sad, sullen little meatballs beyond even the help of ketchup. To be fair to the cook, he probably had little to work with at that point.

I went on deck and took some pictures and saw a "Coast Guard" boat. The first military vessel since the East Coast of the USA. It looked like a U. S. Navy PT boat.

I went inside to my cabin and washed my hands – and won the race with the bathroom fluorescent! I had my hands washed and dried while it was still blinking on!

I spent some time on the porch on the port side – which was toward the harbor. There was regular traffic going in and out, and I saw the little pilot boats speeding to and fro. One hit a wake and I thought it was going over. My impression was that it was one pilot

– one boat. And there were sometimes two boats operating close to each other. Wouldn't it have been more efficient to have more than one pilot on a boat? Probably there's a very good reason why they don't do that, or maybe they do and I didn't realize. I noticed on a map I photographed on the bridge that we were outside the marked "Anchorage Area" along with several other ships. There were so many ships at anchor, they were using the annex.

Supper – grilled beef cutlets, roasted potatoes, rolled-up won-ton. I gave in and zapped it in the microwave. I was getting tired of potatoes that won't melt butter.

The Captain came into the mess in uniform. I said to myself – AHA! – here we go – we'll be in port soon. He usually only put on his uniform when were approaching, in, or leaving port. He upped and asked me if I wanted to go ashore tonight – to Kuala Lumpur. I said no, if there wasn't time to get there the next day, I'd just visit Port Kelang if there was time. I couldn't see arranging for a hotel, packing a bag, etc., and having to view Kuala Lumpur with one eye on my watch and one eye on my camera lens. Better to miss it, unfortunately. Captain said "2300 hours" but whether that's when we would take on the pilot or when we would dock, I wasn't sure. I'd just keep an eye open for when the ship started moving. It sounded like a coffee evening. I was already drinking a Coke from the passenger recreation room fridge. Made a note NOT forget to tip steward the next day.

8:20 PM – we started moving. We had been a bit over 10 hours at anchor, waiting to enter the port. I went to the bridge. It was very dark, with the glow of port in the distance. The Pilot came on. There was an unholy noise of chatter on the various walkie-talkies, in the middle of which, in very American accents, I heard: "How ya doin'?" "Dunno yet." That made me rather homesick.

We finally arrived in Port Kelang. Buy 10:30 PM we were tied up at dock. I went down to the office. The Port Agent – a young man

The World. Around it. On a ship. Mostly.

with a long black beard, and smudges of a couple of colors of something on his face – said I had to go with him. I waited while all the other port paperwork was done and several cartons of Marlboros changed hands. About midnight I went with him to the port office. It was a long drive through the port to a building with a "Soaring Atrium Lobby" in which I had to sit to wait. That didn't do my altocelerophobia any good at all. I got electronically fingerprinted, which went OK, and got a Malaysian Visa stamped in my Passport.

I had noticed that the estimated departure time the next – sorry – THAT day – was 1600 hours. The Port Agent said I would need to be back at noon to allow time for exit processing (Apparently the exit processing would be complicated. In fact, as we walked back to his car, he held out my passport and said "This I keep." Then he handed it to me.) I asked about transport to Port Kelang. It turned out that it was at least a half-hour each way, and up to $50.00 each way. Leaving, when you boil it down, about 2 hours in Port Kelang. For $100 in cab fares. Not a good deal. It looked like the trip to the immigration desk would be my sole experience in Malaysia.

As the Port Agent drove me back to ship, he stopped the car a few hundred yards short of the place the ship was berthed. We just sat there for a while, silently in the dark. I wonder if that was my cue to hand him something? He had been handed probably $400.00 worth of cigarettes in the office, quite openly. Was I supposed to slip him a few thousand Ringgit? I'll never know. After a couple of minutes, we proceeded to the ship. Oh, well – I'd got their stamp in my passport. I was feeling thoroughly strung-out and weird. 1 AM. Bedtime, with the aid of a rare sleeping pill.

The World. Around it. On a ship. Mostly.

Day 46 (41) 7/27/2016 Wednesday

N2° 55.289' E101° 17.213'

Speed 0 kn Heading N/A ^{0}

33 miles from yesterday's position. Av. Speed last 24 hr −1kn. 9447 miles from home.

At dock in Port Kelang.

Not going noplace. The previous day's delay ate up all possible "town time" in either Kuala Lumpur or Port Kelang. It would also make us late to Vung Tau, I suspected. Also maybe Hong Kong. Maybe the best thing would be a walk around the port? I saw a couple of "canteens" while being driven to immigration the previous night. At least I would have the chance to spend some of the Ringgit. At the expected rate, when we passed around Singapore, it would be dark.

Still felt a bit strung-out from, I suppose, the previous night's late night adventure to immigration. Plus the coffee vs a sleeping pill. I hoped I wasn't getting sick.

Took a bit of a morning nap to make up for late night. It helped.

11:00 AM − Decided to try for the Port Canteen. I asked the Captain and he had them call for a shuttle and lend me a yellow safety vest − which I might "forget" to return − and I got my helmet. They are both necessary for going ashore in the port.

A crewman took me downstairs and waited with me for the shuttle. Nice guy − good English. On the way in the shuttle, we passed an ambulance and a bunch of people near one of the cranes. I couldn't see how bad it was. Not our ship. I saw a group of teenagers − all boys − who looked like students getting a field trip to the port.

The World. Around it. On a ship. Mostly.

The Canteen was an older building, right by the canal that parallels the berths. It was three stories high, with a blue canopy down the canal side. It might be the same canteen as in the Maya Jasanoff blog. The shuttle dropped me there, and I went inside. In the main building there were two or three food stands and a small convenience/snack shop.

I looked around a bit, then went to one of the food stands. They served curries. I figured out it was self-serve, with non-throwout plates provided. The man behind counter saw where I was looking on the hot table and said "Potato. That side – vegetables – chicken over there." I scooped up some potatoes – in sauce – and rice – basically fried rice, and several pieces of chicken. Just chopped-up chicken, not like our pieces, in sauce. It was all REALLY GOOD!!!! Of course – the people running the stand were Indian.

It was a very nice, sunny, mild day without the humidity I'd been expecting so I took my plate out on the canopied area, with a bottle of water, and ate. YUM! When I got done, I wondered what to do with the plate. There were no napkins, so my fingers were quite yellow. I saw sinks in the eating area. That's quite common, I believe, in Muslim countries. So where to get rid of plate and the bones? I saw a trash can. Nearby stood a tall, middle-aged Indian man with a great mustache. I started putting the trash in the bin and he stepped up to assist, then took the plate. He was the busboy. He looked like a territorial governor.

I washed at one of the sinks. At a beverage stand I asked if they had iced coffee. He told me "Inside". All I could figure was that he meant the little snack shop. I got a can of "Nescafe" there, sat under the canopy and drank it. I looked around a bit after that and waited for the shuttle. A bus stopped and the students came out. All boys. The only women visible were workers in the food stalls and cleaners. I was glad I got there for lunch before the boys did.

The whole time I was getting looks. I was the only white guy there, and even if not, I would have stood out just by my size and general appearance. Several men got off the shuttle and one pointed me out to the others with an attitude of "Get a load of THIS guy" that needed no translation. I noticed several men carrying baggies with what looked like iced coffee inside. Interesting. Another man sat down near me to wait for the shuttle. Malay, middle-aged, dressed like everybody else in hard hat, vest, etc. The shuttle came and we got up. He looked a bit startled when he noticed me, but seemed to be asking (non-verbally) where I was going. I just pointed my thumb over my shoulder at the ships, and he gave me a come-with-me gesture. When we got in, I said the name of our ship and he said "23." He knew what berth our ship was in. He got off sooner than me, so he wasn't working on our ship. Nice man.

I climbed up the stairs and signed back in. In my room, I noticed in mirror that the beard hairs right below my lower lip were stained slightly yellow by the curry. That's GOOD Curry!

All of that cost me 6.7 Ringgit. $1.68.

On the board in the office departure time was listed at 8:00 pm. If it had been listed that way this morning rather than 4:00 pm, my activities for the day might have been different, but it wasn't a bad day. If we leave at 8:00, it will probably be light out before we get down by Singapore. It will be interesting to see what we see down there. What about Vung Tau? Who knew?

Supper – meatball soup - pork stir fry, orange rice. Salad! We must have taken on a new consignment of lettuce and tomatoes. Now to get tired of vinegar and oil dressing all over again.

We finally pulled away from the dock at 8:45 pm. Oh, well.

The World. Around it. On a ship. Mostly.

Day 47 (42) 7/28/2016 Thursday

N1° 16.975' E103° 17.684'

Speed 19 kn Heading 132°

179 miles from yesterday's position. Av. Speed last 10 hr – 18kn. 9534 miles from home.

40 miles west of Singapore.

The Captain appeared to be hauling ass to the degree possible down the Melacca strait. When we took a left at Singapore (very soon) we'd be up on the port side tires only and then we'll burn rubber toward 'Nam.

I've seen at least a half-dozen Dr. Whos where the trouble is caused by the captain of the space ship refusing to slow down for fear of losing his/her bonus. I wonder if this captain gets bonused like that? I supposed we'd soon be invaded by Cybermen.

We were supposed to be in Vung Tau at 7 AM the next day. To make that would have required an average speed over the next 24 hours of 30 knots. I didn't think the ship could go 30 knots. So we would see.

I went on the bridge after breakfast and took (many) pictures going around the tip of Singapore. It was just after dawn when I got to the bridge, and the sun was not like I had seen on previous dawns, a ball of fire, but a flame – its shape blurred and smeared by the clouds, but fiery and awe-inspiring. The sea was table-smooth and dotted with a great variety of ships and boats. Tankers of all shapes and sizes, fishing boats and floating behemoths like us, some even bigger than us. All were suffused in a mist that made everything a lighter or darker shade of grey.

As we approached Singapore, the sun came out, but everything in the distance was viewed through mist. Ships and boats nearby became very sharp and colorful as the day got rather sunny and hot, but the city itself, and the shoreline, remained unclear and misty. Singapore is a very impressive city, with its tallest buildings seemingly concentrated in a fairly small space. The tallest buildings all looked quite new. The most remarkable was a set of three buildings (which may be considered to be one building, in fact) with a structure joining them at the top which is made to represent a ship. Google "Marina Bay Sands Hotel" to see it.

Rounding the tip of Singapore, there were literally hundreds of ships and boats. Freighters of all sorts, cruise ships, excursion boats (who loved to give their passengers a thrill by cutting right across our bow,) fishing boats and more than a few military-looking patrol boats. Before coming on the trip, I had watched a documentary about piracy near Singapore. It concerned itself with groups of pirates who, using fishing boats, would hijack a fuel tanker and call up a tanker of their own. They would then steal the fuel from the captured tanker and sell it on the black market.

As we left Singapore, there were scores of small tankers at anchor, just the sort to be victims of those pirates. I wished them luck, and was glad to see a small police boat going from fishing boat to fishing boat checking, I suppose, for weapons and such.

Now we were speeding toward Vung Tau at 20 kn. At that rate we would get there 7 PM-ish the next day. We were supposed to get there 12 hours before that. We'd see how much the captain wanted to make up time.

Lunch – chicken vegetable soup, shrimps with heads on, rice pilaf. For dessert, ice cream bar AND flan!

Napped. After the nap, a cadet came to my door and said that at 5:00 PM there would be a drill, would I please come to bridge at that point. A couple minutes later, the Captain called and said same thing. There was an inspector on board whom they wanted to impress with their trained passenger.

The World. Around it. On a ship. Mostly.

The fire alarm went off and I went to the bridge on cue. I looked around – a very smooth sea, completely empty. Good for making time. While the Captain gave drill instructions on his walkie-talkie he told me (big secret) that the Inspector had at one point asked about "The other Captain – not on duty." The Captain realized that he meant me. Apparently I'm good casting for a sea captain. I remembered that a stevedore in Newark had asked me "You the Captain?"

Still on the bridge, the Captain said – "Please go with this officer, get immersion suit and helmet from cabin and go to "Abandon Drill." I got my immersion suit from its cubby in my cabin and on the way downstairs we met the Steward who took my immersion suit and guided me the rest of the way. It's his job to assist passengers. He helped me put on the life jacket. Funny – I got a bit of a claustrophobic feeling putting it on.

We then got counted and taken out onto the upper deck and then up one flight to the lifeboat deck. Fortunately we didn't have to get into the lifeboat. We got instructions – the Inspector was standing by – the officer giving the lecture asked: "Any questions?" Nobody had any so we were dismissed. At 6:00 the crew in was in a debriefing so I decided to wait a while before going down to supper. The Cadet took my picture during the drill, with me in my life jacket and such. I'll ask if I can have a copy. (I asked – never got it.)

So – the sea was smooth and clear, and we were racing for Vung Tau, Vietnam. Just then – an announcement – "2000 will become 1900" – turning the clock back that time rather than forward. Interesting.

Email Home:
```
N1° 16.975'  E103° 17.684'
40 miles west of Singapore
```

The World. Around it. On a ship. Mostly.

Actually, that info above is now out-of-date. That was as of 6 am. It's now lunchtime, and we have looped around Singapore (I took many pictures) and we are currently east of there, (pardon the expression) hauling ass for Vung Tau, Vietnam. Never thought I'd be in a hurry to get to 'nam.
We'll probably be 12 hours late, so no idea what kind of shore time there may be. Maybe none. We'll see.
Seriously, we're really speeding along. We are at or above 20 knots pretty much all the time. We passed a cruise ship, and a couple of frat boys jumped off and started water-skiing behind us. Boy, will their arms be tired!
Actually, around Singapore I did see passenger vessels. One small cruise ship and a bunch of tour boats and water-bus sorts of things. Lots of fishing boats, too, some of which loved to see if they could cross our bow without getting killed. We didn't hit any. I was taking a bit of video of one, and it came very close and cut across our stern. Actually it looked, I expect, very much like what it would look like getting boarded by pirates, and that's

The World. Around it. On a ship. Mostly.

just the place for it. No pirates, though.
So we're speedboating northeast. It will be interesting to see how far we've gotten tomorrow morning.

The World. Around it. On a ship. Mostly.

Day 48 (43) 7/29/2016 Friday

N7° 36.044' E107° 01.815'

Speed 20 kn Heading 10°

569 miles from yesterday's position. Av. Speed last 25 (really) hr – 22.76kn. 9040 miles from home.

225 miles South of Ho Chi Minh City.

Continued to burn rubber for Viet Nam. 192 miles to go - 9 to 10 hours. 9 hours or so late. What that would do to shore time was still unknown.

I had been thinking that living on the ship was a bit like living on the bus when I worked as a road stagehand all those years ago, and last night I dreamed that I was back on the bus. I dreamed that I was waking up and looking out of the window by my bunk and seeing us rolling through a city on the way to the theatre. In the dream I could even tell which city, although that's faded now. I just remember that it was in Pennsylvania. Scranton? Maybe. But certainly the movement of the ship at night was a bit like sleeping on the bus used to be.

The sea was still smooth and it was completely overcast. When I opened the curtain in the morning to put the Garmin on the sill (to get a good GPS reading), I saw several small (fishing?) boats. The closest land was about 150 miles away – the south tip of Viet Nam. An officer on bridge said that there was an island about 40 km away where the boats come from. They need to be at 1000 meter depth for best fishing.

Still roared along at 20 kn. A rough guess was that we might get into Vung Tau closer to 3 – 4 PM.

Lunch – beef vegetable soup – grilled salmon steak – not bad. On the side, finely chopped chicken and veg stir fry and orange rice. Flan.

The World. Around it. On a ship. Mostly.

On the bridge the Captain said we'd get into port at Vung Tau around 6 PM and leave at about 4 AM. There was a fee to go ashore – maybe $25.00. I made a note to ask the Port Agent if there would be any place very close to port to go this evening to get some things (a comb for instance – mine had gone missing. Did I mention that?) and maybe find something to eat.

We docked at 5:35, having come through heavy rain just as we came into port. The rain was so heavy that we couldn't see the navigation lights at the bow. I talked with the Inspector. It turned out he was Turkish, living in Marseilles. I waited a bit then went down to office to see the port agent. I had a feeling I wasn't leaving the ship.

My feeling was correct – not worth the time (what there was of it) and expense. I had an idea – to see if I could manage someday to make a tour of the cities I've missed. Although I don't know if the airline my daughter works for flies to Vietnam. I'll have to check.

Supper on board – some sort of "Chicken Ala King" which was not at all bad. Roast potatoes. Flan.

Email Home:
```
We're still burning rubber for
Vung Tau Vietnam. We'll probably
get there at suppertime or just
after.  We were supposed to be
getting there right about now (7-
ish in the morning.) So what that
means   for   "shore   leave"   is
unknown.   Hopefully  we  will  be
able to make up more time before
Hong Kong. We're supposed to get
there late on the 31st, and leave
in the late afternoon of the 1st.
```

The World. Around it. On a ship. Mostly.

Not much news - the fire and "abandon" drill yesterday was an adventure - I'll tell you all about it. We have an "Inspector" on board at the moment and the Captain is making sure everything is as it ought to be. Looked out this morning at completely overcast, rainy sky and saw dimly in the distance - small boats. I assumed they're fishing boats. The nearest land is about 150 miles away, as near as I can tell, unless there are some small islands that don't show up on the map. That's a long way to be out at sea in a very little boat.
Hope things are going OK there-

The World. Around it. On a ship. Mostly.

Day 49 (44) 7/30/2016 Saturday

N10° 14.288' E107° 09.886'

Speed 18 kn Heading 100°

Miles from yesterday's position – N/A. Av. Speed last 24 hr – N/A. 8865 miles from home.

10 miles south and 5 miles west of Vung Tau, Vietnam.

I didn't go ashore. By the time we were in port in Vung Tau, it was getting dark, it was raining, it was suppertime and I just didn't have the energy to wander out into some strange country, even to eat at a Canteen.

We must have left in the morning closer to 5 AM than 4. Smooth sea, and a chance to get a move on as soon as we got far enough out to be away from the cluster of fishing boats who seemed determined to get in the way. Didn't they know I was in a hurry to get to Hong Kong? Actually, we were scheduled to get in at 11 PM the next day. Even if we got in at 1 AM, that wouldn't have affected my getting to shore in the morning, and may have meant more port time. I'd just have to be sure to nap in order to stay up for the port agent when we arrived.

After breakfast I went out onto the porch – lots of oil rigs in the distance including new ones just being built and 3 ships which were customized for the purpose of oil-rig building and drilling and looked very strange. In the old days they would have inspired tales of fire-breathing sea monsters. They seemed to be drilling. Or something.

Back inside – looking out the window – I saw a distant island that seemed almost a hemisphere, and seemed to be mostly vegetation-covered with a sandy-colored slash from top to horizon. And another, smaller and more distant, to the north. On the wall map, just a couple of nameless dots.

The World. Around it. On a ship. Mostly.

Lunch – grilled pork cutlet, mashed potatoes, small bundle of asparagus wrapped up with a piece of bacon. Once again, even the vegetables had meat. Napped.

Supper was billed as "Burger." Such a "Burger" as made me long for McDonalds. Yep, it was that bad. This time I managed to get it not slathered with sauce, which helped a bit. But seriously. Straight to Portillo's.

Sea very smooth – still tooling along at 20 kn. High hopes for Hong Kong.

```
Email Home:
N10° 14.288' E107° 09.886'
10 miles South and 5 Miles East of
Vung Tau
We got to Vung Tau, Viet Nam
yesterday late afternoon. As we
approached the port, it was sunny,
but I could see in the distance -
inland - a large storm coming. It
was interesting to see how
familiar it looked. It was very
much like, when driving down I-57
or just generally being away from
the city in Illinois, seeing a big
storm rolling in from the West.
The same thunderheads, the same
sheets of rain coming down, the
same slow, ominous progress
forward. Then the leading edge of
the storm comes in, with strong
winds and pouring rain for a few
minutes, then it settles down to a
steady, mild rain. Exactly the
same thing. But in our case we
```

The World. Around it. On a ship. Mostly.

were approaching a major seaport with all sorts of little ships and boats in our path which, for a while at least, we couldn't see. Some were too small to show up on radar. Didn't hit any, though. That rain was one reason I didn't go ashore. By the time we reached port (substantially up the inlet from the town of Vung Tau) it was getting dark and it was raining. The area around the port is fairly dismal, so I didn't feel like exploring there, and there was no time to get anyplace else. So I had supper on the ship, watched some Dr. Who, and went to bed. Some World-Travelling Adventurer.

We're now on our way to Hong Kong, with a fair prospect of getting there more or less on time. I have been in touch with my contact there (We met at the Cornish fest in Australia) and hopefully will get to spend some time with him and his wife - who I haven't met. Lots of fishing boats out the window, but not much else but water.

The World. Around it. On a ship. Mostly.

Day 50 (45) 7/31/2016 Sunday

N16° 06.709' E111° 01.917'

Speed 21 kn Heading 13°

Miles from yesterday's position – 335. Av. Speed last 24 hr – 14kn. 8441 miles from home.

Due east of a spot between Da Nang and Hoi An Vietnam, due south of Maoming, China.

Smooth sea – clear sailing – 20 kn. A fair shot at getting into Hong Kong on time. Some overcast – mostly tall, fluffy clouds. Yesterday an officer on bridge said there was a chance of more rain, but so far, so good.

I looked at the Hong Kong information that I had prepared before the trip in order to start getting ready to go ashore. It looked like I had messed up the currency values completely. I would have to ask. Went out on the port side porch (shadier in the morning) and sat. Not much to see but horizon and birds. In about 2 hours, there was just one boat in the distance.

Lunch – steak, not bad. Fries – cold, but not overcooked. Dessert – "Drumstick." Tripe soup. Like I said, the broth is good. One of the new officers (some came on at Port Kelang) – big, stalwart young guy – opened the lid of the soup tureen, lifted up a ladleful, stopped, looked, sniffed – and put it back in the tureen. He called for his steak to be well-done.

Nothing posted about arrival time in Hong Kong – would check after nap.

I woke up from nap to discover that we were hardly moving, and we were sixteen hours out of Hong Kong. What fresh Hell was this?

The World. Around it. On a ship. Mostly.

Here's what. On the bridge they told me that there was a huge typhoon ("As big as one that kill a few people") at Hong Kong. So we were sitting there "drifting" at a safe distance. For one or two days. DAYS! I emailed my Hong Kong friend as soon as the computer was free. This would screw up the entire rest of the schedule, as I doubted if there will be a chance to make up time any time before the Pacific and even then – TWO DAYS! Oh, well – keep smiling.

Supper – half a plate of elbow macaroni with spaghetti sauce (with carrots in) and half a plate of thing-crust pepperoni and mushroom pizza. Not too bad. They both needed zipping up. I had noticed a jar of Tabasco sauce on the table and put some on. When I opened the jar and smelled it, I got REALLY homesick.

I talked to the Captain – if we had gotten into port in HK before the storm had hit, we would have been forced to go back to sea, even if the loading wasn't finished, because ships can't be tied up at the docks during a typhoon. We would have had to go out into hurricane winds and 11-meter waves. We were better off floating where we were. He said Seattle will probably be delayed. He showed me the storm coming in to Hong Kong on the weather map on his computer. It looked bad. The Second Officer said he has I month left on his contract and then will be eager to get home – he's got a 3-week-old baby.

Email Home:
N16° 06.709' E111° 01.917'
Due east of a spot between Da Nang and Hoi An Vietnam, due south of Maoming, China.
Day 2 of crossing the South China Sea to Hong Kong. Clear sailing on smooth and sunny seas. Just right for making some time - we're

The World. Around it. On a ship. Mostly.

still racing along at about 20 knots. We have a shot at getting to Hong Kong on time, which would be about 11:00 tonight. If so, I may very well be able to get ashore for the morning and part of the afternoon tomorrow. Yesterday - Day 1 of South China Sea - I saw and photographed one of the oddest ships I've seen yet. They're drilling oil wells out by where we were in the open ocean and one of the ships was all derricks, gantries, machinery, cables and a tall rig with flame coming out of the top. If one of those was projected back in time, there would have been reports of fire-breathing sea monsters in Marco Polo's journal. Other than that, not much other than fishing boats and distant ships to be seen.

The World. Around it. On a ship. Mostly.

Day 51 (46) 8/1/2016 Monday

N18° 07.462' E112° 09.166'

Speed 0 kn Heading N/A °

Miles from yesterday's position – 157. Av. Speed last 24 hr – N/A. 8244 miles from home.

262 miles south of Yangjiang, China.

We were still drifting, waiting for the Typhoon to leave Hong Kong. They were probably getting hit pretty bad by it at that moment. We'd probably continue to drift that day and maybe all of the next as well. According to the captain, we were about 13 hours out of Hong Kong. The sea was smooth. It was completely overcast, due, I'm sure, to the typhoon. Hadn't been outside yet, but it felt like there was wind hitting the ship, which figured. It occurred to me that our new passenger was sitting in Hong Kong running up a hotel bill, unless he/she's given up on us.

Lunch – pieces of roast pork and lamb grilled. Cold roast potatoes. Watermelon.

I got a weather report via email from Alice re: the typhoon in Hong Kong. Sounded bad. Made a note to remember to copy it to my thumb drive. We were well-off where we were. Wind seemed to have picked up. I could feel the ship sort of "shudder" from the wind and waves. The sea seemed a bit choppier. Not surprising, I'm sure. It would be interesting to see how long the captain waited after the typhoon passed to head in. We could expect to find some lingering bad weather as we get to HK. We'd have another day of drifting, I supposed. Napped.

Looking out the window at the non-moving water I felt the ship give a rumble in her deepest innards. I thought for a second that maybe we'd start moving, but soon noticed a ghostly, heart-shaped, black vapor cloud floating away. They'd just revved the diesel for a moment to blow out some buildup or some such. No motion. It was almost suppertime.

Supper – roast duck breast – very little meat on it, warm(!) roast potatoes and what looked, at first glance, like potato salad. A cautious bite revealed that the chunks that represented the potatoes were, in fact, raw fish. There were also cucumbers. The steward had worked on the new 3rd mate and got me a bottle of wine.

I went to the bridge – apparently no new info. The man in charge was not the best of the English speakers on board. "Still floating" was what I got out of it. I saw a couple of ships in the distance. I did a quick Garmin check and it looks like, since that morning, we'd drifted about 15 miles south. Looked at the Brag Book again – Homesick? Li'l bit.

> [As an early Father's Day gift, the girls had put together a small photo album with pictures of family, grandchildren, Mary's wedding and other such. They labeled it "Jim's Brag Book." The idea was for me to have it to show other passengers and people I'd be chatting with socially. As it turned out, there was little to do with it other than to look at it myself, but that was reason enough to have it.]

> **Email Home:**
> N18° 07.462' E112° 09.166'
> 262 miles south of Yangjiang, China.
> Drifting. Still sitting here – to 'Drift with the tides and wander with the winds' quite literally. If we drift all day and night – and we probably will – it will be interesting to compare the coordinates and see how far the wind and tide will have moved us. It's good we're here, actually.

The World. Around it. On a ship. Mostly.

We might have got to Hong Kong before the typhoon hit. When I first heard that, I thought - well - then we'd just sit it out at the dock. But that's not how it works, according to the Captain. First of all, all loading and unloading would stop, then, for fear of ships being blown off their moorings in the harbor, the harbor (spellcheck wants me to put a 'u' into harbor) must be cleared of ships. That means that we would have had to go back out to sea literally 'in the teeth of the gale.' We're better off here.

So, the latest estimate is that we'll be here today and tomorrow. We'll see. It's overcast, as you might expect, and though I haven't been outside yet, I have a feeling it's windy. The sea is fairly smooth, however, and no rain as yet. Just a grey day going nowhere. The current tune stuck in my head, not surprisingly, is an old Beatles number (mostly instrumental) called, if I remember right, 'Floating.' Google it to get a sample of the current mood. Alice, Bill and Ed - if you can't place it, you will, on hearing it, say - 'Oh yeah - that one.' It's got a really tasty

The World. Around it. On a ship. Mostly.

George Harrison guitar line in it at one point.
So - no news, really. Wish I had web access to check on the progress of the typhoon. Oh, Well.

The World. Around it. On a ship. Mostly.

Day 52 (47) 8/2/2016 Tuesday

N19° 04.654' E112° 42.175'

Speed 13 kn Heading 15°

Miles from yesterday's position – 74. Av. Speed last 24 hr – N/A. 8178 miles from home.

Due south of Zhaoquing, China. Due east of Minh, Vietnam.

Moving! I got up at 4 AM for Old Guy Stuff and it felt like the ship was moving. I looked out the window and could see moonshine on whitecaps going by.

We were still moving at 6 AM when I officially got up. Not burning up the track at about 13 kn, but better than drifting. We were about 19 hours out of Hong Kong at that rate. I'd see what else I could find out as the day went by. The sea was rough and it looked like we were in for nasty weather. With that thought, I had "Bad Moon Rising" in my head all day. I could see other ships in the distance which was a nice note.

On the bridge – the word was "Maybe tonight." I checked our progress with the Garmin and we'd sped up. At that point our speed looked more like 20kn. At that rate we could have reached HK by 8:00 that night. That was not necessarily a good thing. If they loaded/unloaded all night, we might be ready to leave again at – say – 8:00 the next morning. No shore time in that case.

Lunch – soup – some sort of chicken/lentil. Not bad at all. Grilled chicken cutlet, warm(!) mashed potatoes and what seemed to be creamed mushrooms. Actually not bad. Cantaloupe for dessert – tasteless but inoffensive.

The word on the bridge was that we would pick up the Pilot at 7:30 PM that night and dock at about 9 PM. The original schedule indicated 19 hours in port which would have had us leaving at 4:00

PM the next afternoon. That would mean being back on the ship by 2. Maybe there would be some shore time?

Napped. We were still cruising along at about 20 kn. The sky was brighter. It was still overcast but not as dark and threatening as before. The sea was choppy, but not rough. I wondered if this was going to turn out to be "hurry up and wait." I did a Garmin reading and we were only 39 miles from the center of Hong Kong Island. I didn't know where on the island (or if on the island) the container port was, but 39 miles ain't far. 4:13 PM. Again – for me, getting there earlier in the day today wasn't necessarily a good thing, as it would put more of the port time overnight, when I couldn't use it for going ashore. I had a closer look at the Garmin. It appeared that we were heading around the western end of Hong Kong Island. 4:47 PM – we slowed down to 14 kn. 5:37 PM – 7 kn. Turning due north. 5:52 PM – 5 knots.

Supper – fried breaded fish filet, meatballs, orange rice.

After supper I went to the bridge. It was quite dark, and I could see lights of boats and ships, quite a few of them, all around. There were blinking lights of lighthouses and buoys in the distance, and marker buoys defining the lane into port. In the distance I started to see what seemed to be the lights of the city. Mostly it was fine, rectangular patterns of lights on huge buildings, laced between blacknesses caused by islands between us and the lights. As we got closer, the lights and some shore features became more defined, but still blurred by the darkness and mist.

We started to pass, all on the starboard side, inlets and coves with increasingly large buildings in them, right against the shore. They were all brightly lighted and very colorful. On one headland was a blaze of light which covered the whole top of the point. All at once, it switched off. Turned out it was a large amusement park, which turned out most of its lights at closing time.

The World. Around it. On a ship. Mostly.

We finally got into Hong Kong Harbor, passing by Hong Kong Island and Kowloon. The shore was a mass of skyscrapers with bright lights that made the mist glow. We were fairly well out into the harbor, and between us and the city were hundreds of boats with their lights reflecting in the black water.

Some of the buildings had lights that blinked and moved, but one building, one of the tallest, right in the middle, had a light show going on it, with fast-moving graphics including everything from dolphins to dancing bunny-rabbits. Check it out at www.icclightshow.com.hk. How they do it, I don't know.

The scope of the night view, which included a panoramic look at Hong Kong Island, Kowloon and bits on either side of those, was magnificent. Garishly-lit skyscrapers against a jet black sky, with a livid glow all around it from the lights and mist. Never to be forgotten. We slipped beneath a huge bridge and were immediately in the container port.

At 9:43 PM we moored at the dock. I went down to the office and talked briefly with port agent. I noticed on the board that the estimated time of departure was 12 noon. I would have to be back on board by 10:00 in the morning. That's just about when I figured I'd be going ashore. So – no Hong Kong. I knew it could happen, but I sure was hoping to get ashore, see my friend, buy some souvenirs, do the SIM card thing, etc. I hoped that I could manage to get ashore somewhere! Now watch, I thought – there will be delays and we'll wind up leaving at 6pm or some such.

This part of the port (and the rest of it that I could see) was empty – due to the storm, I expect. Another ship was coming in right on our tail.

Email Home:
N19° 04.654' E112° 42.175'

The World. Around it. On a ship. Mostly.

Due south of Zhaoquing, China, Due east of Minh, Vietnam

First of all, on reflection, I think the name of that old Beatles tune was 'Flying', not 'Floating.' But, more importantly, We're moving again! I woke up at about 4am (because I'm an Old Guy) and it felt like the ship was moving. I looked out the window and could barely see some whitecaps going by. We're still moving at 7:30 am. Not too fast - about 13kn, but moving, and toward Hong Kong at that.

The weather, as you can imagine, is not good. Probably it will get worse as we approach Hong Kong. It's raining and windy, and the sea is a bit rough. Looking ahead, it looks like we're in for nasty weather. (Now I'll have 'Bad Moon Rising' stuck in my head all day!)

Here's a cell phone question - In order for my phone to work in Hong Kong, I'll have to buy a SIM card and install it. I also wonder if that same SIM card will work in the other Chinese ports up to and including Shanghai? Any thoughts? I'd google it if I could. The only other port after China will be Pusan, Korea, and I've been told that there will probably be no

The World. Around it. On a ship. Mostly.

shore time there, so no need for a Korean SIM card.

Of course, how much, if any, port time there will be after all of this delay is not yet determined. Also, I will probably not be flying home from Seattle on the 20th, but more likely the 21st or 22nd. I will know better about that in a couple of weeks.

Day 53 (48) 8/3/2016 Wednesday

N22° 20.388' E114° 06.904'

Speed 0 kn. Heading N/A

Miles from yesterday's position – 241. Av. Speed last 24 hr – N/A. 7931 miles from home.

Hong Kong Harbor.

So once again I sat on the ship looking at one of the world's most exciting cities across the cranes of a container port. Actually, this was the first time I could actually see the city, but it sounds better that way. Technically, at 7 AM I suppose I could have left the port for an hour or maybe two, but to go where and do what? I wouldn't ask my friend to get up that early and come get me, and I had no idea what to tell a cab driver. Besides which, even in Hong Kong, the shops probably wouldn't have been open yet, and there wouldn't have been time to do much of anything. This was in the cards. It was entirely possible that I wouldn't get ashore at any of the ports in Asia. That was always possible, but I didn't like to believe it likely. But there we were. Oh, well, 4 to go, including Shanghai.

We took on a new passenger. I had heard the Port Agent say he would pick him up at hotel that morning. Nobody picked me up at my hotel. Probably they carried his luggage on board as well. Oh, well.

In the morning, the port was about full. They must have had a busy night after we got there.

I took pictures from the bridge. It was very misty, and the fog softened the sharp edges of the city. Even now, liking at masses of modern buildings and mechanical monsters like container-port cranes, the mist lends a look like old Chinese paintings. Perspective and depth perception is flattened, and boats float in

The World. Around it. On a ship. Mostly.

vertical space, not in distance. Distant hills and the buildings on them are not farther away, just higher. At a distance, the city is silent and hangs like a vast theatrical backdrop behind the industrial fuss and bother of loading a container ship. Somehow it is now hard to imagine entering that scene. How can one take a cab into a painting? How can one order a meal in a woodblock print?

Not too far away, in the midst of a dense, vast forest of tall, new apartment buildings was a green hill. Green, with small regular shapes covering it from top to bottom. Through binoculars, it turned out to be a cemetery. Chinese cemeteries are very different from ours, with each grave being a small temple or shrine, in traditional style. It may have been very old, perhaps established when that hill was far distant from the city, which grew up around it. A very striking image.

How fortunate to have a platform – the ship's bridge and its outside "wings" – as a 150-foot-high observation and photographic platform. It certainly gives one a chance to view one's surroundings from a more all-encompassing viewpoint.

When I went down to my room I met the new passenger getting his safety tour from Raphael. Name "Ah - long?" Accent – French? I hoped they would post a new list of crew and passengers soon so I could get his name right. Snuck a look at his passport down in the office – "Alain." Turned out he was from [A major French city] and worked at a University. Seemed like a nice guy. He would only be going as far as Pusan.

After we left Hong Kong and were at sea again, I looked out the window and saw another ship going by. It turned out to be the Christophe Columb, the one that Maya Jasanoff was on when she did her blog. It's the new kind, with the "castle" forward and the stack aft. Small world? It was going the other way, and fairly

The World. Around it. On a ship. Mostly.

close, so if I had looked 30 seconds earlier or later, I wouldn't have seen it.

At 9:55 pm we moored at the pier at Yantian. Port agent says ETD is – get ready – midnight the next day! All day to go ashore! Something would surely screw it up!

```
N22° 20.388' E114° 06.904'
```
Email Home:
```
Hong Kong Harbor.  Well, my luck
with  time  in  port  continues,
unfortunately.  We got into Hong
Kong late yesterday evening and I
went down to the office to see the
port agent and get my passport
looked at.   While there, they
posted  the  Estimated  Time  of
Departure for the next morning
(this morning - Wednesday.)The ETD
was noon.  Anyone going ashore is
expected to be back on the ship 2
hours before ETD which is 10:00
am. No time to get anywhere or do
anything.  Too early to ask my
friend to pick me up and anyway -
to do what and go where? Even in
Hong Kong, the shops probably
aren't open that early. Oh, well -
there are 4 more ports, and one is
Shanghai.  There's hope.
We're getting a new passenger this
morning.  Last night I heard the
port agent say that he would be
picking him up at his/her hotel.
Nice. I wish somebody had picked
```

The World. Around it. On a ship. Mostly.

ME up. They'll probably carry his luggage on board, too. Pay no attention - just grumpy. Coming into HK last night was fascinating. Hopefully some of the pix and video I took will do it some justice. I'll try to get some more on the way out, in daylight. Not really depressed or despondent - just griping a bit.

The World. Around it. On a ship. Mostly.

Day 54 (49) 8/4/2016 Thursday

N22° 34.497' E114° 16.914'

Speed 0 kn. Heading N/A^0

Miles from yesterday's position – 53. Av. Speed last 24 hr – N/A. 7920 miles from home.

Yantian Harbor, China (Peoples Republic Of.)

There was a major re-organization of containers in progress, with the (probably temporary) result of there not being any containers directly outside my forward windows. The way things looked, though, that would probably not last. Weather looked good so far (hear that weather gods? I said SO FAR!), about 50% cloudy/sunny, and the clouds didn't look threatening.

So – if all went well – I might be going ashore soon. I'd have breakfast and go down to check both email and ETD, but looking at the containers at that point, it would be some time before they will be done with those, and the previous night the officers were talking to the port agent about various tests and inspections, including the idea of divers. None of that stuff would happen quickly, so hopefully the ETD of midnight would hold. That would mean that I wouldn't have to be back until 10:00 pm. Adventure time! I looked out my relatively clear forward view and saw some very grey, threatening skies. We'd see. Looked out again – it was raining. Then it wasn't raining.

Had a bigger-than-usual breakfast, dressed for shore leave and went down to the office. I got my passport (with Visa!) back from the Third Officer along with a "Green Card" which would get me through various immigration turnstiles. I bought a SIM card for my phone from one of several "Businessmen" (as the officers called them) who were allowed on board – at the boarding area – to peddle their wares, spread out on the deck.

The World. Around it. On a ship. Mostly.

This guy was working out of his briefcase. I didn't really know if the card would even work, but I did my bit, I bought it and gave the number to the sign-out guy. I partnered with Raphael and The Kid (the Cadet) in a cab. The cabs are run by a company well-known to the crew and officers and are licensed to pick up and drop off right at the ship. Also they are not expensive. They are run through a shop called Suzy Seaman's Shop. It's a shop in the thick of town that seems to be one of those "If you want, we got it, if we don't got it we'll get it" sort of places, and I have a feeling that they can get just about anything, licit or il-.

Mostly I walked around town. I had eaten a large breakfast because I wasn't sure if I would be able to get any lunch. Of course there are thousands of places to eat in Yantian. But do you know how say – "How long has that chicken been dead?" or "Can I have mine without eyeballs, please?" in Cantonese? Didn't think so. Yantian is NOT set up for tourists. Almost no English signage, and nobody speaks it. Fair enough, of course, why should they? But it's not convenient.

For example – one thing I wanted to do was to buy a pocket comb. I couldn't figure out where to go to buy a comb. I went to all of the sorts of places you're now thinking about in terms of "Dummy – you should have just gone to a ….." Whatever sort of place you're putting at the end there, I went to one. No combs. Again – do you know the Cantonese word for "Comb?" Didn't think so.

So I mostly walked around for several hours. And sheltered from the rain. It drizzled most of the time, relieved by one big downpour, featuring the loudest and sharpest thunderclaps I've ever heard. Also Yantian isn't big on "Public Conveniences." Ask me no questions and I'll tell you no lies.

I saw street-level sectioning of recently-deceased foul. I saw little shops selling miscellaneous sorts of goods, such as junk-level electronic and electric items, piled randomly in a store front. Most of the businesses were storefronts. Some sold lumber and home improvement supplies. An interior-décor shop was fabricating chrome trim pieces right on the sidewalk. A large fruit stand was being raided (?) by the police (at least 10 cops) and their sidewalk merchandise was being impounded. There were construction projects everywhere.

It was all recognizable and non-bizarre, but about 90° off normal (my normal). People doing things that people do, but within a different set of givens. Also, there was this enormous, grey-bearded, long-grey-haired apparition stalking around, dripping wet, frightening the children and stampeding the goats. Wait – that was me. I sometimes find a sort of Heisenberg Uncertainty Principle in affect when I wander around like that. It's hard to observe the people when, by my mere presence and oddity, I become the focus of attention. The kids were actually amused, and the only goat I saw was on a sign at the front of a restaurant. I wonder what they serve there?

> [I realized that where I was and what I was seeing was basically the "Drive By" stuff. You know – when the shuttle bus picks you up at the airport and takes you through town to the hotel or resort and you drive by all those funny little places where those funny little people do all of those funny little things.
>
> "Oh Roger! Did you see what that man was doing? Cutting up a pig, right there on the street! No, I didn't see that girl. Really, Roger, if you're going to assume that every woman you see is a …..well I, for one, am not here to have dirty fantasies. I'm here to learn about a new culture…..OH MY GOD! That child had no pants on and his mother was letting him pee right on the ……."]

So I finally got back to the ship – and put on dry clothes. Literally "Home and Dry." Interesting experience. The China Visa was a great value. It got me basically waved through Immigration both ways. Next stop was Shanghai – hopefully, I would go ashore there too. Maybe it would be more tourist-friendly. But I was glad

The World. Around it. On a ship. Mostly.

I got off at Yantian. I didn't get mugged or hustled or pickpocketed, and it was very interesting.

After supper – 7:30 – one of the "Businessmen" was still spread out on deck with his watches, game controllers, DVDs and such and one of the crew was buying.

> **Email Home:**
> It's 8:00 in the morning here in Yantian, China. We're going to be here till midnight. I can go ashore! Adventure time! I think I'll buy a comb. I lost mine a couple of weeks ago and this is the first chance I've had to replace it. Thrills - Chills - The Excitement of World Travel!

The World. Around it. On a ship. Mostly.

Day 55 (50) 8/5/2016 Friday

N22° 35.833' E116° 36.166'

Speed 22 kn. Heading 51°

Miles from yesterday's position – 150. Av. Speed last 24 hr – N/A. 7897 miles from home.

237 miles due west of Kaohsiung, Taiwan. In the Taiwan Strait between Taiwan and mainland China.

Smooth sea entering the channel between mainland China and Taiwan. Mostly cloudy, but the clouds didn't look threatening. We were tearing along at 20 or so knots. Somehow we managed to make up all or most of the time lost recently, but nonetheless, we were speeding north to Shanghai.

Next stop Shanghai, then Ningbo. I noticed on the map that we would be passing Ningbo on the way to Shanghai and then apparently doubling back to Ningbo before continuing north to Pusan. Strange.

Lunch – meatball soup, lamb chop, roast potatoes, and something that seemed a lot like black pudding. Not a favorite. I Showed Alain around the deck. Napped.

Supper – roast chicken – dark meat only – mashed potatoes (warm!) and shredded cabbage with bits of onion and sausage. Not bad.

> [It was nice to have someone else at the table at meals. Alain could speak English quite well, and was a good conversationalist. I never got the feeling that he looked down on me for not being French.]

The World. Around it. On a ship. Mostly.

Day 56 (51) 8/6/2016 Saturday

N27° 47.125' E122° 57.465'

Speed 18 kn. Heading 43°

Miles from yesterday's position – 535. Av. Speed last 24 hr – 22 kn. 7395 miles from home.

138 miles east of the mouth of the Feiyun Jiang River, China. East China Sea.

Sunny – smooth sea and ride. My best guess was that we'd get into Shanghai around suppertime and most of our port time would be overnight. We'd see.

Lunch – bean soup with crunchy beans, salmon steak, orange rice.

I saw the Captain and the Chief Engineer in the elevator and the Captain said "Alongside 2:00 in the morning" meaning that's when we'd dock at Shanghai. Later than I thought, but we were still off-schedule and might have to wait for a berth. I could easily imagine that we'd "drift" a bit outside Shanghai. We were still going about 16 knots (at 1:00 in the afternoon) but maybe we'd have to slow down later.

> [In re: elevator. Every article I had read referred to there being an elevator in the Accommodation, but that the writer eschewed its use and always took the stairs. Well to hell with that. I often went down using the stairs, and up a deck or two, but for anything other than that, I took the elevator. I paid a lot for the trip, and I was going to get my money's worth.]

Supper – pork and liver stew.

I went up to the bridge at about 7:30 PM. The bridge was, as always at night, dark. There were the lights of dozens of ships all around. We were still going about 11kn, and I heard the captain radio for pilot information (didn't hear any response) but I was willing to believe that it will be 2:00 AM before we would tie up.

The World. Around it. On a ship. Mostly.

Time ashore? Who knew? I did a Garmin reading and it looked like we were about 50 miles off shore, heading for Shanghai. At the current rate, it would be one-ish at least before we would get that far. So the idea of a 2:00 AM dock time was not too bizarre.

[One of my favorite things was to go up to the bridge as we entered port, especially if it was dark out. The progress was slow enough that there was plenty of time to look and wonder. The bridge lights were always off so as not to impede the view forward. Usually we seemed suspended in a dark globe, with small lights glowing in the near and far distances.

Sometimes the lights were stretched out in a line horizontally across our forward view – the far shore – and a reddish glow would mark our harbor. Sometimes patterns of lights would resolve into the shape of a ship or boat as it neared. Near enough, and we could see into and onto the decks of the ship and see tableaux of shipboard life – mostly men standing and looking up at us.

As we entered one harbor at night, it looked as if we were floating through a vast parking lot, and all of the cars had their lights on. Although we couldn't see the boats, it must have been fishermen using light to entice the fish toward the surface. And the night entrance into Hong Kong will be in my memory forever.]

Email Home:
N27° 47.125' E122° 57.465'
138 miles east of the mouth of the Feiyun Jiang River, China.
Not much to report today - We're heading up the coast of China, and have now reached the East China Sea north of Taiwan. We're still a long way from Shanghai, and may well reach there this evening. That will mean that most of our in-port time will be overnight, so maybe not much if any time to go

The World. Around it. On a ship. Mostly.

ashore. One thing I was going to mention a few days ago- Alice/Mom/You had sent me a blog from Prof. Maya Jasanoff (Is that the right name?) about her trip on a freighter. The other day I happened to look out of my window and noticed a CMA CGM ship heading the opposite direction from us, fairly close by. Because of our relative speeds, it was only in sight for about a minute. I noticed that it was the Christophe Colomb, the same one she was on. Small world.

Again - not much in the way of news-

Counting the days-

The World. Around it. On a ship. Mostly.

Day 57 (52) 8/7/2016 Sunday

N31° 22.560' E121° 34.642'

Speed 0 kn. Heading N/A^0

Miles from yesterday's position – 258. Av. Speed last 24 hr – N/A. 7189 miles from home.

Shanghai.

I woke in Shanghai harbor. After breakfast, I checked the Estimated Time of Departure. It was "1430" – 2:30 in the afternoon. Normally we would have to be back 2 hours before ETD, making it 12:30 at which we would need to be back on the ship. Marginally enough time to make it worth it going ashore. Then Alain noticed that there was an extra notice: "Shore leave expires 4 hours before ETD." Meaning that we would have to be back by 10:30 am. Not enough time available to make it worthwhile going ashore. Oh, well.

I confirmed this with Raphael and he said that it was because of a problem in Yantian when the departure time was moved earlier and some of the crew didn't properly get notified and get back at the new deadline. Something about their Philippine phones not working correctly. So the Captain bumped the end of today's shore leave earlier to avoid problems. I wondered if it will be the same in Ningbo and Pusan. Of course, those are ones where the Captain had said, basically, "Don't bother." So my going ashore days might be over. I don't mind really, Yantian was rather intense and will do me for a while. I had hoped to bring home all sorts of exotic souvenirs, but I expect I'll be forgiven. But we'll see.

Lunch – small steak and fries. "Drumstick" for dessert.

From the ship in the container port, the downtown skyline of Shanghai was clearly visible. I made a point to take some pictures

The World. Around it. On a ship. Mostly.

as I was fairly sure that at least one of the new, tall buildings in sight was very famous, and I may have even seen a documentary on TV about its construction. It turns out that it was Shanghai Tower, which is at the moment, I believe, the second-tallest building in the world. It's the twisty-looking one. The Shanghai world Financial Center is right next door and almost as tall. It's the one with the hole through it near the top. There's another one in sight, which seems to have a huge ball near the top. The Oriental Pearl Tower, I believe.

Shanghai Harbor was perhaps the busiest we had seen. Broad, and with a wide mouth at the ocean end. As far as one could see up and down, there were various sorts of ports. Container, bulk, petroleum and even automotive. Seeing some car-carriers unload finally revealed to me what those odd-looking ships were that I saw everywhere. I speculated as to what this harbor must have looked like during WWII. Clogged with naval traffic and, at times, black with the smoke of bombardment-lit fires. I looked up some pictures after I got home, and such was indeed the case.

When it was time to depart, (about 2:30 PM) we backed out of the berth with the aid of tugs and stood parallel to the ship traffic. It was remarkably like merging into traffic on the Interstate. When a large enough hole seemed to be coming along, we pushed forward and joined the line. There were ships of all sorts and sizes, and we just jostled our way into the stream of ships heading out to sea. In fact, it was organized very much like a highway in that there was a clearly-defined line of ships heading out (ours) on the right, and another clearly-defined line of ships going in on our left. Very dense traffic, huge volume of vessels.

Short nap. On the way to Ningbo – would probably reach there that evening.

The World. Around it. On a ship. Mostly.

Supper – pizza – a 3rd different style – thick crust pepperoni. Not bad. With a piece of chicken on the side that may have been an oddly-cut drumstick or a very large wing segment.

It looked like we'd reach Ningbo fairly late.

```
Email Home:
N31° 22.560' E121° 34.642'
Shanghai.
First of all - Happy Birthday
Alice!   Have  a  nice  time  at
Sergio's!   We're   in   Shanghai,
having arrived in the wee hours.
I see that our Estimated Time of
Departure  is   2:00   in   the
afternoon.   It's 7: 40 in the
morning now.  Normally we have to
be back on the ship 2 hours before
the  ETD,  meaning  12:30.   But
there's  a  further  notice  that
'shore  leave'  expires  4  hours
before ETD, meaning 10:30.  Not
much time to get ashore.
We'll see -
```

The World. Around it. On a ship. Mostly.

Day 58 (53) 8/8/2016 Monday

N29° 53.364' E122° 03.420'

Speed 0 kn. Heading N/A°

Miles from yesterday's position – 128. Av. Speed last 24 hr – N/A. 7264 miles from home.

Ningbo, People's Republic of China.

I guess that I didn't have to say "People's Republic of" China, it just felt kind of cool to do it.

Woke in port at Ningbo – sunny – would find out about port time after breakfast. I doubted if there would be any time to go ashore.

It turned out to be just like the previous day. ETD was 2:00 in the afternoon, and the rule about being back 4 hours (and yes, it did apply to passengers as well as crew) before ETD was in effect, so we would need to be back at 10:00 am. It's 7:30 am now. The port agent said that it was 1 hour each way to and from town, and that might not have included the time to get processed out of the port. So no going ashore at Ningbo. The last chance would be Pusan, Korea.

In a way, I wasn't terribly disappointed, as my main focus had recently become, more and more, getting home. That's not to say that I was miserable and "over" the trip, and I would have enjoyed going ashore if it had been possible, but home's charms and attractions were calling more loudly every day.

In Ningbo harbor I saw the first military ship I'd seen since Charleston. It was a small ship – probably not as big as a Destroyer, but a Navy (Chinese) ship nonetheless. Saw another smaller one later.

Lunch – grilled slices of beef – roast potatoes – mushrooms in cream sauce. Pound cake with chocolate syrup for dessert.

The World. Around it. On a ship. Mostly.

Nostalgic. We used to have pound cake with whipped cream and chocolate sauce for dessert occasionally at home.

Short nap anticipating 2:00 PM cast off.

I went to the bridge at 2 PM. Nobody there. The cranes were still working. We cast off about 3:00 pm. On the way out I saw a Hanjin ship that reminded me of a picture I took in San Francisco by the Golden Gate Bridge of a huge container ship – from the Hanjin Line – entering San Francisco Bay. The ship today was called "Hanjin Spain." I'd have to check the picture from San Francisco once I get home to see if it was the same ship. Also I saw another Evergreen ship I'd seen before. One called "Ever Chivalry." Looked like we were chasing each other around China.

> [I checked, and it wasn't the same Hanjin ship that I'd seen in San Francisco. However, within two weeks of returning home I saw an article saying that Hanjin was filing for bankruptcy and its ships were being refused entry into ports all over the world. I was very glad I hadn't booked the trip with Hanjin!]

Supper – (brace yourself, or skip the next bit if you're squeamish) – kidneys. Meatballs on the side, and orange rice. Actually, I think that the meatballs were there to make the kidneys look good. Even the French guy couldn't finish the kidneys. Tasteless cantaloupe for dessert.

Sea seemed a bit rough. Probably high winds.

```
Email Home:
N29° 53.364' E122° 03.420'
Ningbo, People's Republic of China

I guess I don't really have to say
'People's Republic of' China, but
it feels kind of cool to say it.
I didn't go ashore in Shanghai,
nor in Ningbo for basically the
```

The World. Around it. On a ship. Mostly.

same reason - we arrived very early in the morning and most of the loading and unloading happened overnight. Our departure time was 2 or 2:30, and the rule about getting back to the ship four (no longer two) hours before departure time is still in effect, for passengers as well as crew. Plus, this morning the port agent said that it would take an hour to get to anywhere worth getting to, so there was quite literally no time.

The last chance to go ashore will be in Pusan, and there's no telling what the time will be like there.

I'm not too upset about it, having gotten ashore once in Yantian for a fairly long time. Mostly I'm looking forward to crossing the Sea of Japan, and then the Pacific, and getting to Seattle. And then home, of course. We will see exactly what date I'll get to Seattle. Too early to try to predict at this point.

No news - just routine life on board. We'll be leaving Ningbo in about an hour.

The World. Around it. On a ship. Mostly.

Day 59 (54) 8/9/2016 Tuesday

N31° 40.360' E125° 34.826'

Speed 17 kn. Heading 46^0

Miles from yesterday's position – 243. Av. Speed last 24 hr – N/A. 7075 miles from home.

Due east of Wuhu, China. Due south of Gongzhuling, China.

I used those coordinates mostly because of the name "Wuhu."

Sky mostly sunny, horizon clear, sea calm.

Lunch was a sort of Carne Asada without the spices. Not bad, though. Roast potatoes, and cold onion rings. Watermelon – seedless.

We were making good time. The sky was cloudier, but the weather was mild. Not too rough. I went on deck for a while.

The sea had been as empty that day as it was in the middle of the Atlantic. Interesting – right off the end of Japan, heading for Korea, you'd think there would have been more traffic.

Supper – a sort of chicken ala king with mashed potatoes. Shrimp with heads on on the side. Watermelon.

After supper I went to my room, looked out and saw land. It was Tsushima Island, owned by Japan. It was good to see Japanese territory. I went to the bridge and stayed for a while and saw the Japanese coast guard patrolling, as we were right between Japanese and Korean waters. We got closer and closer to Pusan in the dark, but no pilot showed up. Finally at one point we basically stopped and waited. I went to bed.

```
Email Home:
N31° 40.360' E125° 34.826'
Due east of Wuhu, China. Due south
of Gongzhuling, China.
```

The World. Around it. On a ship. Mostly.

I mostly used those coordinates because of the name 'Wuhu'.
We're on our way to Pusan, Korea. My calculations show us getting there in the wee small hours of tomorrow morning, and, since we will probably be in port around 12 hours, there will probably be no time to go ashore. The 4-hour return rule is still in effect.
At Pusan the other passenger leaves, bound, apparently, for Sri Lanka. I'll be on my own again for the remainder of the trip. It's still too early to say precisely which day I'll be flying out of Seattle. The current, original schedule would have us arriving in Seattle late on the 19th and I would disembark on the 20th in the morning and go straight to Sea-Tac airport. But over the next week-and-a-half, the date will probably change, and change later, to the 21st or 22nd. It all depends on how fast we can get across the Pacific.
I keep hoping that they will announce something like 'We are going to make an extra stop in Osaka' or something like that, since we will be (are) so close to Japan, but it probably won't

The World. Around it. On a ship. Mostly.

```
happen.   I'd settle for Yokohama.
But we added a stop in Charleston,
so I can still fantasize.
No news - just routine shipboard
'life.'
```

The World. Around it. On a ship. Mostly.

Day 60 (55) 8/10/2016 Wednesday

N35° 04.110' E128° 48.988'

Speed 0 kn. Heading N/A⁰

Miles from yesterday's position – 298. Av. Speed last 24 hr – N/A. 6738 miles from home.

Pusan, South Korea.

Mostly cloudy.

Only 128 miles from Japan. I suppose that's not the most respectful way to identify a spot in Korea, but I've got memories in Japan, and Korea is just another container port. I bet myself that there will be no time to get ashore. The same formula – into port in the wee hours of the morning, have 12 or so hours in port (mostly used up overnight when I was asleep), have the 4-hour rule in effect (thanks crewmen, whoever you were) – town a long way from port – all equaling no port time.

Alain departed that day – I'll miss our chats, which were mostly me answering questions about the USA. At one point, for example, he said that a friend had told him that, legally, in the USA and in Britain, a person was considered guilty until proven innocent. He wanted to know if that is true. Seriously. I was glad to set him right on that one. I will miss his saying "It was very parteekoolare" when he meant "It was very peculiar." So back to solitude. Well, that's partly what I was there for.

True to form, we got in in the early morning, and our ETD was noon the next day, meaning that shore leave ended at 8:00 am. Oh, well.

I was feeling bad about not having fancy Asian souvenirs to bring home to the family, but on the only day I might have got them, it was in a place where I had no idea how to go about it. I suppose I could have managed, but the whole experience was so overwhelming(?) disorienting(?) that as I said, I couldn't even manage to find a pocket comb. Maybe I'd buy some things at Seattle airport and treat it all humorously. In any case, I believed that I'd be forgiven.

[I was.]

I found that while I was reading in my cabin, a card had been slipped under the door. A simple "Goodbye" from Alain. Later I ran into him on the bridge. He'll be heading out about 11 AM, it seemed.

Lunch – breaded and fried fish. I saw the cook (new guy?) cutting up a fish earlier and I thought he was slicing steaks off a salmon, but maybe it was some other sort of fish and that's what we just had. Boiled potatoes (first time for that) and shredded cabbage stir fry. Tasteless cantaloupe for dessert.

At nearly 1 PM we were waiting to leave. The cranes were up and raised. I wanted to see this cast-off as it will be the last one I would see.

We cast off about 2:00 PM, leaving Korea and heading back into the Sea of Japan. In the radio chatter on the bridge I would have sworn I heard an American voice mention "Iceberg chunks." I saw another Hanjin ship that reminded me of the pic in San Francisco by the bridge. This one the "Hanjin Italy"

Supper – roast pork – not bad, a little dry, roast potatoes. We turned the clocks ahead at 6:00 this time. The sea was almost glassy, and there were few other ships and boats.

Before leaving home, I had told the senior grownups that, if there was bad news while I was gone, I preferred to have it as I traveled, rather than them waiting until I got home to tell me. I would abominate them having to carry that around with them – the "Dad still remains to be told" idea. I could picture being taken aside at

The World. Around it. On a ship. Mostly.

O'Hare, to some secluded bench, and told the terrible news. I hoped that that wouldn't happen.

There would be challenges to face for all of us in the months to come, I was sure, but I hoped that nothing horrible was waiting for me when I got home. Both for my sake, and for the sake of those keeping the agonizing secret and having to tell it.

[No such thing happened. Whew.]

Email Home:
N35° 04.110' E128° 48.988'
Pusan, South Korea.
Last port before we head across the Sea of Japan (presumably) and then across the Pacific (definitely). We got in in the wee, small hours again, and the Estimated Time of Departure is noon today. It's now 7:20 am, and shore leave expires at 8:00 am. Oh, well. I had hoped to arrive with arms full of exotic items for everyone, but, as you recall, on my one day ashore, I wasn't even able to figure out where to buy a pocket comb. Still don't have one.
The other passenger left today - wasn't at breakfast, so I presume he left early, as I will probably do in Seattle. As I said, it's too early to accurately predict which date we will get to Seattle Plus there's the date line.
But at noon or so - we'll push off and the next stop should be the

The World. Around it. On a ship. Mostly.

USA and then home. I'm still enjoying being on the ship, etc., but I'm also eagerly anticipating seeing all of you and sleeping in my own bed.

The World. Around it. On a ship. Mostly.

Day 61 (56) 8/11/2016 Thursday

N37° 21.918' E133° 25.269'

Speed 22 kn. Heading 53°

Miles from yesterday's position – 301. Av. Speed last 24 hr – N/A. 6518 miles from home.

Due East of Nagaoka, Japan. Due North of Kochi, Japan. Middle of the Sea of Japan.

Very smooth sea – little to no visible traffic. Morning haze, but otherwise looked like it would be clear. We were too far from either coast (Japan and Korea) to see land.

I realized that I'd done all of the tasks for which I put reminders on that day's calendar page by 8:09 am. Now what would I do for the rest of the day?

For one thing, I went to the bridge. The sea was absolutely flat calm, a bit hazy but generally clear. There was a nice cool breeze. I didn't know when I'd known such fresh, clean air. The wind was coming, I believed, from the north, and there's not much up there, all the way to the Arctic Ocean, to mess it up. Except us, of course, but I was ahead of the stack. I just stood there breathing it in in big gulps. I'm glad that I haven't done anything (like cigarettes, for example) to ruin my capability to take big, deep lungfuls of air, when the air is this good.

Coming back to the cabin, the steward had been, and had sprayed air freshener and used scented cleaners. I opened a window to get some of that good air in. No icebergs. I probably heard that wrong. I wished that I had internet, so I could have googled "Iceberg. Sea of Japan."

I went on deck. It was very pleasant at the bow. Quiet and serene. Back at my room, I opened another window to get some cross-ventilation. And maybe flies.

Lunch – "Steak on a Stick." Beef chunks with peppers and onions roasted on skewers. Fried rice. Some sort of cold cauliflower salad. "Drumstick" for dessert. The steward has expressed his approval of the new cook, and explained (I think this is what he was explaining) that this fried rice was <u>real</u> fried rice and involved no food color. Was this the end of Orange Rice? One could only hope. Napped.

The phone in my room rang and I was informed that there was to be a fire drill, but it was not necessary for me to come to the bridge. The alarm went off – a warbling tone over the PA, but this time my window was open and I got the ship's horn as well. Scary loud. A few minutes later there was an announcement that there was also an "abandon" drill – much more elaborate – but I took the info that I didn't have to go to the bridge for the fire drill as permission to skip the abandon drill as well. I hoped I was right.

Supper – whole boneless breast of chicken stuffed with a light creamy sauce – somewhere between mayo and hollandaise, but neither one, wrapped in a slice of bacon. Potatoes which seem to have been stir or pan fried after boiling, and mixed veg. As Mark Twain would have said "Now, this is something LIKE!" Much better food with the new cook. Was this the end also of Pork and Liver stew? We could only hope. Some sort of pastry for dessert – brought a piece to room and will report later, if it's worth reporting on. It seems to have bits of either orange or carrot in. Pastry was tasty.

```
Email Home:
N37° 21.918' E133° 25.269'
Due East of Nagaoka, Japan. Due
North of Kochi, Japan.

All Japanese references today.
We're in the Sea of Japan. I
```

The World. Around it. On a ship. Mostly.

noticed on one map it also said, in parentheses: '(East Sea)'. Some people must not like calling it the Sea of Japan for some reason. The sea is, appropriately enough, in a state of Zen-like calm. Really. You could roll a ball across it and it would go straight ahead and not bump on anything.

Also - at breakfast, they've started putting out bread (for toast) in those large, perfectly square slices like we had at breakfast in Kyoto all those years ago. Very Japanese, especially considering that we haven't landed in Japan at all - regrettably.

Sometime tomorrow we will go through the strait in the north of Japan (the name of which escapes me at the moment) and head out onto the Pacific and thence to Seattle. The strait is narrow enough that I should be able to see both islands - Hokkaido and (I hope this is right) Honshu.

No news - just sailing along smoothly-

Day 62 (57) 8/12/2016 Friday

N41° 38.375' E141° 30.781'

Speed 20 kn. Heading 80^0

Miles from yesterday's position – 534. Av. Speed last 24 hr – 22.5kn. 6023 miles from home.

Tsugaru Strait, Japan.

I had hoped and expected to reach the Tsugaru Strait sometime later in the morning when there would be more light. The strait is fairly narrow, and I would have been able to take pictures of Japan on both sides of the ship. To my considerable surprise and disappointment, when I looked out my window at 6:00 AM, the last possible visible headland at the eastern end of the strait, on the southern side, was receding as a gray hulk into the morning mist. The Captain's haste to make up lost time had put us through the strait in the very early hours. I supposed that I must appreciate his desire to get us to Seattle ASAP, but that was another part of the trip I was genuinely looking forward to, and it was sacrificed to the delays we had experienced over the last couple of weeks. All part of freighter travel, of course, but DAMN!

Depending on our exact course, a bit of Hokkaido might be visible off the port side at about 11:30. I'd have to watch for it. Cold comfort, even so. The idea of someday taking a flying trip to the places I've missed was getting more attractive.

So we were finally in the Pacific. Just had to get across it and – home!

The steward was not at breakfast – that was a first. Hoped he wasn't sick. (Turns out he was OK – he was working on something else and forgot.) Both the 3rd Officer (yesterday) and the 1st Officer (this morning) assured me that I will have the movies that day. We'd see….

The World. Around it. On a ship. Mostly.

I went up to the bridge to see the tip of Hokkaido go by. I saw that, and a LOT of dolphins. Some appeared to be surfing just under the surface of the waves. It pointed up how clear the water was there. I may have gotten 1 or 2 good shots and a bit of video. With the dolphins was a boat with "Research" painted on the side. The question was – was the boat there because of the dolphins, or were the dolphins there because of the boat? It was good to see at least a bit of Japan in the daylight. The coast was hazy, but a few buildings could be made out. The area on the Southeast cost of Hokkaido is not densely populated. The nearest town appeared to be Kashiwanocho, which delivered 0 entries when I googled it. [At home – after the trip. In fact, just now, while I'm editing this]

Still, the coastal mountains pushed up out of the clouds and caught the sun. Very scenic. I may have said that I have memories in Japan. When I and my former wife got married, we soon after visited friends of hers in Japan, where she had spent time as a student. We had a wonderful time, being hosted by some of the nicest, most hospitable people I've ever had the pleasure to meet. We saw mostly the area around Tokyo, Kyoto and the Inland Sea, so a very different part of Japan than the Tsugaru Strait, but Japan nonetheless.

Lunch – bean soup (beans weren't crunchy!) Pork stew (no liver!) Rice. I believe I'm going to like this new cook! The 3rd Officer brought the thumb drive to my room with 6 movies on. All American, 2 with Sylvester Stallone. All were one sort of action movie or another.

Supper – BBQ chicken – dark quarter. I'd swear it was done outside on a grill. Fried potatoes, eggplant in wide strips, battered and fried. Food had definitely taken an upswing. Very foggy out.

Email Home:
```
N41° 38.375' E141° 30.781'
Tsugaru Strait, Japan
```

The World. Around it. On a ship. Mostly.

Having come through the Tsugaru Strait, we're now officially in the Pacific Ocean. Next landfall - Seattle!
I realize that these updates have become something of a Litany of Disappointment, but here's another. I had calculated that, at a normal speed, we'd reach the Tsugaru Strait sometime this morning, about 11:00 or so. It's a narrow strait, and I would have been able to see and photograph Japan on both sides of it. As it happened, the Captain is in a rush to make up lost time, and, when I looked out my window at 6:00 this morning, the last headland of the Strait on the Eastern side was receding as a grey hulk into the morning mist. So, sorry - that's another bit of trip I won't be able to bring home. The idea of a flying trip to see bits I've missed is becoming attractive!
So we're on our way to Seattle. Once again, can't specify the date we'll get there, but, at the rate we're going, I'm sure that the intent is to get there as scheduled, in the evening of the 19th. If so, I'll sleep on the ship and head for SEA-TAC airport

The World. Around it. On a ship. Mostly.

in the morning. My eager anticipation of seeing all of you again is far outweighing any annoyance caused by our messed-up schedule. Spirits are high and I'm counting the days!

The World. Around it. On a ship. Mostly.

Day 63 (58) 8/13/2016 Saturday

N44° 55.147' E151° 27.778'

Speed 20 kn. Heading 66^0

Miles from yesterday's position – 551. Av. Speed last 24 hr – 23 kn. 5518 miles from home.

Due east of Changchung China. Due south of Zyrjanka, Russia.

Still extremely foggy. Thought about icebergs a lot. We were tooling along at 20 or so kn. I was assuming and hoping that icebergs show up on radar.

I went to do laundry. Neither machine on F deck (my deck) would start – I had trouble like that before, but not both at once. I went down to E deck and only one of the two would start.

Looked like, including that day, it would take eight full days to get to Seattle. I'd wait until after the Date Line to guess what that date will be. The Date Line thing I still hadn't worked out. Would we set our clocks back a day or ahead? I supposed if I thought about it enough, I could figure it out. But then, if I turned out to be wrong, what a dummy I would feel. And yes, I know it has nothing to do with Time itself. Just with the frame of reference by which we measure time. We wouldn't actually lose or gain a day.

The computer we use for email was in its second day of "Out of Order." I hoped they'd get it fixed soon. I felt like volunteering to look at it, if not. As if I could have done anything. But I'd have felt better having tried. I asked the captain and he said I could use one of the office computers for email. Dear ob'm.

   [That's a Cornish expression. It means "Dear of him"]

Lunch – breaded beef cutlet, roast potatoes (cold), carrot salad. On the bridge- just a bright haze outside. I couldn't see the bow nor the water from there. The radar shows nothing at all nearby, and

The World. Around it. On a ship. Mostly.

the Captain says that icebergs are all north of the Aleutians. We'd stay south of them. The Aleutians.

Supper – shrimps with the heads on (again.) This time, though, the little legs had been removed and they seem to have been somehow deep-fried on a skewer, or something. Not nearly as distasteful, and more tasty, that way. Beats me why it's considered cool to cook and serve their heads. Unless some people eat the heads. If so, I don't want to know about it. Rice. Shredded beets, which remained on my plate. Hate beets. For dessert – some sort of baked thing (Cornish readers, if any – it looked a bit like Flapjack) with chocolate icing. I brought a piece to my room and would try it later. It was tasty.

Nearly 8:00 PM and we were still in the fogbank. It was just as thick as it has been all day. Thank God and (Note to self – look up inventor's name) Heinrich Hertz for Radar.

```
Email Home:
N44° 55.147' E151° 27.778'
Due east of Changchung China. Due
south of Zyrjanka, Russia.
Continuing    east    across    the
Atlantic.  We seem to be taking a
northerly route.
Yesterday  I  did  manage  to  see  a
bit more of Japan, as we passed by
the     southernmost     point    of
Hokkaido.  Not much of a view, but
it   was   nice   to   see   Japanese
ground.
Plus - there were dolphins!  I saw
a  boat  -  looking  like  a  tugboat -
with  'Research'  painted  on  the
side,  and  nearby  it  -  and  us  -
```

The World. Around it. On a ship. Mostly.

were a large number of dolphins jumping. I got a couple of pictures worth showing.

Late yesterday we moved into a fog-bank, and we're still in it at lunchtime today. On the bridge, it's all a bright haze outside and from there you can't see the bow of the ship, or the water. I looked at the radar, and there's nothing nearby. The Captain says that all icebergs are north of the Aleutians. Presumably we're staying south of them.

I count that it will probably take 8 days to get to Seattle, but that's not official. What with the Date Line, I'm not sure what date that will be. I'll keep you posted as we get closer.

No other news.

The World. Around it. On a ship. Mostly.

Day 64 (59) 8/14/2016 Sunday

N47° 41.802' E161° 44.474'

Speed 20 kn. Heading 73°

Miles from yesterday's position – 528. Av. Speed last 24 hr – 23 kn. 5022 miles from home.

Due east of Jiamusi China. Due south of Kamkatka, Russia.

Still in heavy fog. We'd been in heavy fog for 1000 miles and more at that point. I've spent weekends in a fog before, but this is getting ridiculous ('atsa some joke, eh, Boss?) It must have been really boring for the guys on the bridge. Radar showed nothing nearby.

We still seemed to be on a sort of arched course, with the arch going north. Maybe the fastest way, given the globular nature of the surface on which we were traveling. I'd have to look that up. Depending on how far north we arched, we might hit the dateline the next day, where the Dateline zigs to the left to get the Aleutian Islands in the same date as the rest of Alaska. If we wouldn't be far enough north for that, probably one more day.

Lunch – small steak, done medium, fries – best I've had on the trip, corn on the cob – not too bad. Tripe soup seemed to have survived the change in cooks, unfortunately. Must have been a big favorite with somebody. The broth is good, though. "Drumstick" for dessert. Napped.

Supper – pizza. Pepperoni. Thick crust. Not bad. Another baked thing for dessert. Brought one to the room.

While I was in elevator after supper there was an announcement. What it seemed to say was "Tomorrow will be Sunday." I couldn't hear announcements too well in the elevator. Well, that day was Sunday so I figured it was the date line thing. The next day would be the same date and day of the week as today. I checked on the

The World. Around it. On a ship. Mostly.

bridge and yes, at midnight we don't change the hours on the clock, just the date and day of week.

As far as the "lose a day/gain a day" thing: All along we had been, every few days, changing our clocks ahead, skipping an hour. 5:00 became 6:00, for example. "Losing" an hour every time. Well, at midnight we get 24 of those hours back. Why didn't I figure that out for myself? It's like one of those Sherlock Holmes mysteries that's "Perfectly Obvious Once Explained." (Quoting myself.)

In the evening – set everything back to Saturday, August 13 so it would all click over to Sunday August 14 (again) at midnight, and we could all have another nice Sunday.

```
Email Home:
N47° 41.802' E161° 44.474'
Due east of Jiamusi, China. Due
south of Kamkatka, Russia.
Still in a heavy fogbank. That
makes nearly 48 hours in a
complete fog. I've had weekends
like that in a figurative sense,
but this is quite literal. I wish
I could see some sort of on-line
weather map to get an idea of the
extent of this 'pea soup', but –
no internet.
We're still arching northeast. I
suppose the northward part is due
to some navigational necessity,
bit every mile north gets us
closer to icebergs. Did I mention
that the visibility is zero?
There's radar, however. No serious
danger.
```

The World. Around it. On a ship. Mostly.

If we continue northward, we'll cross the date line tomorrow, where it juts west to keep the Aleutian Islands in the same date as the rest of Alaska. If we don't go that far north, it will be day-after-tomorrow, I expect. Not terribly important, but that will put me on the same date as you all, and it will be easier to communicate about dates of arrival and such. Also - there's very little else to talk about in these updates.
What have I seen lately? Fog.
What have I done? Laundry. See?
Ah, the excitement of world travel.

Day 65 (60) 8/14/2016 Sunday (Again – courtesy of The International Date Line)

N49° 34.335' E173° 59.297'

Speed 20 kn. Heading 81⁰

Miles from yesterday's position – 579. Av. Speed last 24 hr – 24 kn. 4508 miles from home.

Due east of Nianzishan, China. Due south of a point between Ozero Vaam Ecgyn and Oljutorskij, Russia. (Really. I'm not making those up.)

Happy Sunday – Again! We turned the clocks back a day at midnight, and it was Sunday, August 14th, 2016 all over again. My rough calculations showed that we might reach Seattle sometime on the 18th, but we were into some rougher seas, plus the original schedule said the 19th at 6:00 PM, so I was still betting on getting into Seattle on the 19th and flying home on the 20th.

Once it had happened, the date line adjustment made perfect sense.

Last night and this morning, the bathroom fluorescent didn't light up at all – just blinked. At breakfast, I asked the steward about it, and he tapped the shoulder of a strapping young lad who turned out to be the Electrician. I told him about it (at about 7:15 or so am) and at 8:23 am, one of the crew had just left my room, having replaced the tube. Those guys are good!

I got out the suitcases and started packing things I wouldn't need in the next few days. Felt a bit weird. I wonder how "Institutionalized" I had become?

I went to the bridge and asked Gamal if there was any new word on arrival in Seattle. He said, and showed me in an official schedule from the Company, that we would get to Seattle on August 20th at 8 AM. That would mean I might be able to fly out on Aug. 20th in the afternoon or evening, or stay one night at an

The World. Around it. On a ship. Mostly.

airport hotel and fly out on the 21st. I would communicate with home about this. I supposed that they would have to make the hotel reservation if needed, given my lack of phone or internet.

OK – so how much sense did this make? The day before, the steward had come in and changed the sheets and towels and cleaned the room, as he does every Sunday. Then, the next day, he came in and did it again. Because it was Sunday. But he had just done it the day before, and it was normally done once a week. Strange.

Lunch – bean soup with non-crunchy beans! Actually it was a bit like chili. Just a bit. Whole boneless chicken breast battered and baked. There was something I wasn't crazy about in the batter, but the chicken was fine. Fried potatoes and some sort of green pepper salad. Not bad.

The Captain confirmed an 8:00 AM arrival on the 20th, and even said that's the anticipated "along side" time, not when we'd pick up the pilot. It was looking better for flying on the 20th. Napped.

I had noticed on map that, depending how far north we would arch in the next day or so, we could be technically in the Bering Sea. I'd have to compile a list of the different Oceans and Seas and such we've been on. So far, it looked like this: Atlantic Ocean, Indian Ocean, Strait of Malacca, South China Sea, Taiwan Strait, East China Sea, Sea of Japan, Tsugaru Strait, Pacific Ocean, Bering Sea, Strait of Juan de Fuca, Puget Sound. That's sailing the 7 seas, if you count oceans as seas. I do, got a problem with that?

Actually, they all look pretty much the same.

At 5:00 PM, the announcement came that it was really 6:00 and the clocks started advancing.

Were they getting a bit lax with the announcements? It caused some confusion in the mess because they hadn't been told. I went down at the new 6:00 and steward told me come back in 45 minutes. About a half-hour later he called me and told me they were ready.

Supper – sliced roast beef, roast potatoes and some sort of amorphous, grey cold mass that must have involved mushrooms, cream sauce, onions and something green. And a blender. Surprisingly tasty. "Pancake" for dessert. Had it before – crepelike objects made of possibly rubber, cold. Skipped it this time.

An officer clipped to my door a thumb drive with movies. A random assortment, perhaps there would be a good one in there. I put them on my laptop to watch later.

> **Email Home:**
> N49° 34.335' E173° 59.297'
> Due east of Nianzishan, China. Due south of a point between Ozero Vaam Ecgyn and Oljutorskij, Russia. (Really. I'm not making those up.)
> So it's Sunday 8/14 again! We just had that yesterday!
> We made the Date Line adjustment last night, when all of the calendars were set back 24 hours. The time stayed the same, we are simply doing Sunday 8/14 over. I have had many days for which I would like a do-over, but I didn't do anything I particularly regret yesterday. A missed opportunity, but what would I do on the ship? Now that it's happened, it's perfectly obvious how it works. All along, every couple of days, we have turned the clocks ahead 1

The World. Around it. On a ship. Mostly.

hour, essentially losing an hour each time. We just got 24 of those hours back in a lump. Simple, really.

My calculations of time and distance show that we could reach Seattle on 8/18, meaning that I could fly home on the 19th. However, for one thing, we have just encountered some rougher seas, which may slow us down. It's still almost completely foggy, but, what with Radar, that hasn't delayed us. The other thing is that the printed schedule, which we have been behind for weeks, shows us getting into Seattle on the 19th, at 6 PM. My best guess is that the Captain will want to conform to that schedule. that's just my opinion at this point, and I'll provide more specific and official details when they are available. I know that in order to arrange for flights, info is needed as early as possible. I'll do my best to provide it, but for now, it looks like I'll be flying on the 20th.

See you all soon!

The World. Around it. On a ship. Mostly.

Day 66 (61) 8/15/2016 Monday

N50° 45.818' W174° 15.655'

Speed 20 kn. Heading 79°

Miles from yesterday's position – 531. Av. Speed last 24 hr – 23 kn. 3982 miles from home.

Due west of Burke Channel B.C. Canada. Due south of the middle of Atka Island in the Aleutians.

The Garmin said we were in the Bering Sea. That even sounded cold. About halfway between Japan and Seattle.

We were no longer in dense fogbank, but it was still completely overcast. I stuck my nose outside, and it felt like Chicago winter. Went to the bridge – not much to see, just clouds and grey water. Came back to F deck and went out on the porch outside my cabin. I felt a poem coming on – here it is:

> Spindrift
>
> Spindrift flies off whitecaps casting lace nets on the icy blue-green waters
> of the Bering Sea.
>
>
> The swell breaks, its tip blown back by the wind and snow-like spray jumps, turns to mist
> and falls.
>
>
> Our ship's wake pushes the waves back on themselves, just as the wakes of the whalers' ships, the explorers', caused the spindrift to dance.
>
>
> Their faces, like mine,
> felt the distant ice, the farthest North.

The World. Around it. On a ship. Mostly.

They, too, came inside to take off the chill
and tasted the sea-spray on their lips and mustaches.

Not so long ago.

Here endeth the culture. Like the font? It's called Footlight MT Light.

I felt chilly after all of that and put on my hoody. The air vents still seemed to be blowing cool air (yes, I had them closed.) It seemed like they'd want to turn on the furnace for a few days. Hey – BERING SEA!

Lunch- sliced beef in a tomato sauce with potatoes. Not bad. Beef-noodle soup, not bad, shredded carrot salad – no comment. Tasteless tinned pineapple for dessert.

I went to the bridge, and noticed the lack of other traffic. The Radar was completely empty. Quite a change from, for example, Singapore.

At 5:00, I heard the clock start advancing. Then came the announcement; "1700 becomes 1800." Just like yesterday. A bit lax re: announcements. I figured I'd wait a bit to go to supper in case the time change is a surprise to the galley like it was yesterday. Steward called about 6:25 – they were ready to serve supper.

Supper – roast chicken – dark quarter, rice, red cabbage salad.

Email Home:
N50° 45.818' W174° 15.655'

The World. Around it. On a ship. Mostly.

Due west of Burke Channel B.C. Canada. Due south of the middle of Atka Island in the Aleutians.

All North American references! We're about halfway between Japan and Seattle. Today we will pass north of Hawaii. WAY north. We're actually, briefly, in the Bering Sea. That even sounds cold. I haven't been outside lately, but I may go today, just to say I've braved the icy blasts of the winds of the Bering Sea. Sounds like a Stan Rodgers song.

We're not in solid fog at the moment, but it is completely overcast. Not sunny and tropical like it was for so much of the trip. After this, I'll be glad to swelter in Chicago for a while, just to thaw out.

No further data re: arrival, just that we're due in (at the dock - 'alongside', as it's put - in fact) at 8:00 the 20th, meaning that I probably could make a plane in the afternoon or evening. Again, if it's necessary to stay over until the 21st to get a flight, I will gladly do so.

Looking forward to being home and taking my car to the shop. Wait - that's not the part I'm looking forward to.

The World. Around it. On a ship. Mostly.

Day 67 (62) 8/16/2016 Tuesday

N51° 49.909' W162° 30.927'

Speed 20 kn. Heading 83°

Miles from yesterday's position – 514. Av. Speed last 24 hr – 22 kn. 3478 miles from home.

Due west of Dean Channel B.C. Canada. Due south of Thin Point Lake, Alaska.

On my Garmin map it looked like Thin Point Lake (named, I suppose, after a Sharpie®) is about the last point on the peninsula hanging down from Alaska before it starts breaking up into the Aleutian Islands. Actually I wrote that because I'm so proud of how every time I type Aleutian it doesn't slap spell-check all over it. Why I know how to spell Aleutian, I don't know.

Rainy, overcast, foggy, medium-rough sea. Our heading was now more like 92° which means that we'd started arcing down again, toward Seattle. "Ladies and Gentlemen, we have begun our initial descent into Seattle. In preparation for landing, please be sure your seat backs are....."

Lunch – pork cutlets in sauce – good. Mashed potatoes warm enough to melt butter – good. Brussles sprouts – not bad. Napped.

I thought that the weather was starting to clear, but at 5:00 pm it was windy, foggy, raining and cold.

Supper – shrimp with the heads on, deep-fried this time. Not bad once you get the heads off. What is it with the heads, anyway? Rice. Some sort of cabbage, green pepper and onion stir fry. Not bad. A bit of a kick.

It was still rough. Actually, there were some of the highest waves I'd seen so far. By comparison to some I remember from before, and the height the Captain estimated those waves to be, these could have been 5 meters high. Earlier, on the bridge, an officer had told me that the weather forecast for Seattle was not good.

While checking email, I saw sitting by the computer a sheet of paper with a food order that will be picked up in Seattle. It had on it: "Pig Blood-frozen." First of all, I was glad that was for an order that was going to be consumed after I was off. It sounded like they were performing some sort of bizarre rituals. Either that or it will go into the recipes. If it had been on the last order as well, I was rooting for the rituals.

Email Home:
N51° 49.909' W162° 30.927'
Due west of Dean Channel B.C. Canada. Due south of Thin Point Lake, Alaska.
We're starting our downward arc into Seattle. Still looking at the morning of the 20th to arrive. I know that thoughts have begun about flights - It just occurred to me that, especially if my arrival at O'Hare will be at an awkward time, we could do the same sort of parking thing as we did when I left. Someone could park my car in the long-term lot a day or two before, text or email me the location, and I, upon arrival, could get myself out to the car and drive home. I have a spare key with me to open the door and turn on the ignition. If that would be

convenient, it's OK by me. Let me know.
The only flaw in that plan as stated is that I don't have with me the keys to my place. Whoever would leave the car in the lot would have to stash my regular set of keys in the car so I could get in once I got home. I believe that you could lock the car with the keys stashed.
Nothing going on here - it's cold, rainy, cloudy and foggy. I've begun to pack, for lack of anything much else to do except read. I'm glad I loaded up my Kindle!

Day 68 (63) 8/17/2016 Wednesday

N51° 31.546' W150° 07.766'

Speed 20 kn. Heading 94°

Miles from yesterday's position – 537. Av. Speed last 24 hr – 23 kn. 2970 miles from home.

Due west of Burke Channel B.C. Canada. Due south of Turnagain Arm, Alaska.

The sea was calmer, but we were still rolling quite a bit. It was hazy, but the overcast seemed to be breaking up. I had a hard time sleeping the previous night, lots of rolling and banging. I looked out my window at about 2 am and saw a great full moon and reflections and clouds. I took pictures. In the process, I finally learned how to control the ISO number on my camera. Can we go

The World. Around it. On a ship. Mostly.

back to Hong Kong so I can take some more pictures? At night? I was trying hard not to think about all of the pictures I could have taken if I had figured out the ISO thing earlier. Leaving New York, for example. ARRRRRGH. Nighttime. Statue of Liberty. Verrazano Narrows bridge. GRRRRRRR.

They seemed to be power-washing the exterior of the "Accommodation." I couldn't tell if the water on the windows was from that or from the rain. I went up to the bridge. It was rain.

The rolling must have been more pronounced than previously. Out of my room's front windows, I could see, very close up, the ends of containers. They were noticeably swaying at a slightly different rhythm and angle to the window, due, I suppose, to the design of the ship and the decking they sat on. I never saw that difference before, even on previous rough days.

Lunch – small bacon-wrapped filet steaks. Two of them. Fries – good. Mixed chopped salad vegetables in a dressing – too cucumber-intensive. Napped.

Supper – some sort of breaded cutlet – I strongly suspected veal – with a fried egg on the top. I ate the egg. And the fries. Surprisingly, they were real, properly cooked French Fries. Pretty good. Plus some sort of slaw, of which I didn't care for the dressing. I brought the dessert to my room – something baked and chocolate-iced.

Part of the problem with supper at that point was that it had been coming at the almost-daily time zone change. At 5:00, the clock started moving forward and they announced "1700 will become 1800 – Good appetite." Not much appetite for supper at 5:00. Oh, well – only 2 more days.

Email Home:
N51° 31.546' W150° 07.766'

The World. Around it. On a ship. Mostly.

Due west of Burke Channel B.C. Canada. Due south of Turnagain Arm, Alaska.

Weather's still medium-bad, rolling a lot, although the sea is calmer.
Still cloudy and misty.
It's still looking good for arrival in Seattle on Saturday morning about 8:00 am. We'll coordinate on flights soon, I'm sure. I have taken my phone off airplane mode and, as soon as I see some bars (not today or tomorrow, I'm sure) I'll sent a test message or something.
Just a warning of sorts - my hair is now longer than most of you have ever seen it. I'm torn between going up to Mediaeval Times and getting a job as King Arthur or putting on a black sweatshirt and doing 'An Evening with George Carlin.' Future hirsute prospects - unknown. Just so you know.
Counting the days - on the fingers of one hand!

The World. Around it. On a ship. Mostly.

Day 69 (64) 8/18/2016 Thursday

N49° 40.858' W137° 58.533'

Speed 20 kn. Heading 108°

Miles from yesterday's position – 553. Av. Speed last 24 hr – 24 kn. 2466 miles from home.

Due west of Strait of Georgia B.C. Canada. Due south of Alsec River, Alaska.

Cloudy, not raining, sea fairly smooth.

I did laundry for the last time. The washers on my deck were still not working so I went one deck down.

Looked at my map – at the rate we were going, we'd be about 200 miles from Seattle at 6 AM the next day. That meant maybe twelve to fourteen more hours into Seattle, so we'd be getting there the next day (Friday) in the evening.

Earlier I asked the captain if we were still due in on Saturday morning and he said yes, but he also said some other things I didn't catch. In any case, it looked as if I would disembark on Saturday morning. Very soon. Strange. I hoped things would go well with flights. My plan was to go straight to the airport unless I heard anything to the contrary soon. Maybe the next day we would be close enough to land to get bars on the phone. I don't mean to call pubs and/or taverns. I mean that there might be cell phone coverage.

Lunch – potato soup. Slices of stewed beef in gravy. Mashed potatoes. Stewed carrots. "drumstick" for dessert. All good.

On the bridge, the Captain told me a story (in his charming Eastern European accent) about something that had happened to him once in a port. He told me it was "off the record" so I won't tell the story here, but he emphasized the veracity of the story and that it had happened to him personally by saying "It is copypaste of mine!" I think he was aiming for "copyright" and missed.

I told him about my plan to leave the guitar on board. He was appreciative, as several people on board played. He mentioned the Chief Engineer, who looked rather musical, with his long chin beard and man-bun. He was, according to the Captain, "composer."

> [You may recall that I bought a guitar at a pawn shop at our last American port. I didn't play it as much as I thought I would, and bought it partly because family and friends couldn't believe that I was not taking one of my guitars with me. I was glad to have it, and used it a few times, but I didn't want to take the trouble of getting it home. So I wrote a "Letter of Gift" and left it on the ship for the enjoyment of the crew and officers. It went like this:
>
> Letter of Gift
>
> I give this guitar to the ship (the name of the ship went here), for the pleasure and entertainment of her crew and officers, present and future, in thanks for the wonderful experience I had on (the name of the ship went here), in the summer of 2016.
>
> I recommend that the guitar be kept in the crew recreation room so that it will be available to the crew members and officers at all times.
>
> I hope that this guitar will sail on the (the name of the ship went here), for years to come, and will bring enjoyment and relaxation to all of the seafarers who sail on her.
>
> Jim Wearne]

Supper – pork cubes roasted on a skewer – good. Rice. Fried strips of breaded eggplant. Tried them the other day – not a big eggplant fan. Dessert – a donut. Brought it to the cabin and to try later. Tried it. Not good.

When I had last checked my email, I found an itinerary from the airline as arranged by Mary for my flight home. It was an

The World. Around it. On a ship. Mostly.

afternoon flight on Saturday with a connection, but that was just fine. Actually the afternoon nature of the takeoff was a good thing, in that I wouldn't have to panic getting to the airport and would, I hoped, have time for some lunch there.

The wine box was almost empty. I felt that it was my bounden duty to finish and it would be most efficient if I were to empty it that night. Actually, I'd already started, which may necessitate some editing before this particular entry is ready for the presses. More editing than usual, I mean. Especially as I was still getting my allotment of one glass of wine at supper. There was also the remains of that bottle of Irish whisky. (Oops – I wasn't going to mention that!) It promised to be an interesting evening. I was just celebrating my penultimate evening on the ship. Sue me.

[Yes, I know words like "penultimate." I went to college.]

The World. Around it. On a ship. Mostly.

Day 70 (65) 8/19/2016 Friday

N48° 27.591' W128° 48.972'

Speed 12 kn. Heading 90°

Miles from yesterday's position – 428. Av. Speed last 24 hr – 18 kn. 2037 miles from home.

192 miles due west of the mouth of the Strait of Juan de Fuca.

I had a hard time sleeping the previous night, in spite of the wine. For my last night, I'd probably make an exception and take a pill. I expected that I'd be too excited and too full of what I'd do the next day to sleep much, otherwise. The sea was rougher, but the sky was clear. There was some rolling. I just then realized how rotten it would have felt if the Captain said – "Well – we've got to drift outside of Seattle for a couple of days......"

I went on deck for the last time. It was quite windy and crewmen were power-spraying the stern. I only went to the bow.

Lunch – chicken soup, salmon steak. Roast potatoes. Brussels sprouts.

I sent message to Mary to test my phone. I saw some bars, but also an exclamation point. I couldn't connect to Facebook. Probably we were still too far from land.

I went to the bridge. It was nice and sunny. Vancouver Island was off to port. Did I see snow caps on some of the mountains? I saw a whale go across the bow. Took some selfies. Napped.

Supper – roast chicken, dark quarter. The steward left the bottle of wine on the table. There was too much left in it to finish off, unfortunately. Oh, well.

I went to the bridge to see us go into the Strait of Juan de Fuca. I saw whales! Lots of them! It wasn't sunset just yet, and there was light enough to see that there were several pods of whales all around us. They didn't get as close as I would have liked, but the sea was fairly shallow there so that they stayed near the surface. Mostly I saw splashes with a head or tail in them, or a broad, grey back rolling up out of the water. For as far as the eye could see, there were puffs of water spraying up ten feet or so above the surface, as the whales blew.

As we drew nearer to the mouth of the Strait of Juan de Fuca, snowcaps glowed in the now-reddening light from the west. One of the officers said to me "Welcome home."

We'd be several hours getting to port, too long to stay up. I hoped I would sleep.

So ended the sea voyage. The next day, up and to the airport. And home.

> **Email Home:**
> N48° 27.591' W128° 48.972'
> 192 miles due west of the mouth of the Strait of Juan de Fuca.
> The problem with not having Internet is that now I want to Google 'Juan de Fuca' and find out why he's got a strait named after him and I can't.
> Mary has worked her usual wonders and I've got flight info for tomorrow (knock wood). I'm half afraid to refer to getting off tomorrow and flying home for fear that the Captain will say - 'Looks like we've got to drift outside of Seattle for a couple of days.....'
> The sea is a bit rough, but the sky is clear as we head under the

The World. Around it. On a ship. Mostly.

(hopefully) sheltering influence of Vancouver Island. Alice - as we pass the many islands in the straits between here and the port, I'll be remembering that restaurant ('The Farmhouse?') and how wonderful it smelled walking in, after the drive and ferry ride to get there. I don't remember what we had, but it was a great meal, as I recall.
So - to finish packing and such, and (again - knock wood) get ready to disembark tomorrow morning.

The World. Around it. On a ship. Mostly.

Day 71 (66) 8/20/2016 Saturday

N47° 35.007' W122° 20.766'

Speed 0 kn. Heading N/A

Miles from yesterday's position – 329. Av. Speed last 24 hr – N/A. 1727 miles from home.

Seattle Container Port.

I woke – 6 am – to the announcement "Everybody to come to ship's office for face check." It was Passport Control. Down in the office, a US official in a flak jacket first made me go to the end of the line because "I have to use a different set of stamps." He then made it sound like I was some sort of vagrant or idiot when all that was at issue was me getting a shuttle to the terminal gate, then a cab. "We can't have you wandering all over the terminal!" The Port Agent – a pleasant young lady – said that would be no problem, she'd be around a while to make the arrangements. The US Official reminded me of the Monty Python line: "It's folks like you what causes unrest!" Really – of all of the officials I had met and seen on the trip, he was the only one who made me want to punch him in the throat. "Welcome home," indeed.

After breakfast, I made sure that I was all packed, and let the folks at the ship's office know that I was about to disembark. A crewman helped me get my bags off the ship (hooray!) and I walked over to a small port security office and stood waiting for the shuttle which would take me to the front gate. It felt strange to realize that I would not be getting back on the ship. There were a few people I wanted to say a proper goodbye to, but saw very few of them, and those were busy. Our Captain was getting off as well, and was to be replaced by the lady Captain who had taken us from New York to Savannah. It was good to see her again.

At the front gate, a chatty young security man and I talked while the taxi came. It was good to have a conversation with a native

The World. Around it. On a ship. Mostly.

English speaker again. It had been over two months since my last one, and, not to appear prejudiced, it was nice to be able to use idioms again.

The cab left me at Seattle International. I went in and found a 3-hour line at the front desk. I needed to go there because of my status as a stand-by passenger and parent of an employee of the airline. Also to check my big bag. When I had been standing in line about fifteen minutes, I began to wonder if I were about to pass out, and if I should sit on the floor for a bit. Then I realized that what I was feeling was "sea legs." The entire airport was, as far as I was concerned, pitching and rolling like the ship. Disconcerting, but I could handle it once I realized what it was.

> [Actually, that effect lasted several weeks, gradually lessening in intensity. In fact, it's now exactly a month since I got home, and I still feel it a bit sometimes. The funny thing is that it's not a feeling of movement from side to side, but up and down.]

I got on a good flight after having some lunch. Actually I made for the first place I saw in the airport that might make a decent cheeseburger. Yum.

As we ascended out of Seattle, I realized that I was seeing the container port out of my window, and our ship! Not enough time to get a picture, unfortunately. It was good to see her once again like that.

Flying east from Seattle, there were beautiful snow-capped mountains, and huge plumes of smoke from a forest fire. I got out my camera.

This next bit deserves its own paragraph. It is about a Miracle. When I tried to take a picture of the forest fire, my camera wouldn't turn on. Just dead. Nathan shakin'. I changed batteries. Nada. Once home, I googled and found that that is a common problem with those cameras due to some fault in the manufacturing. It could happen at any time, and was fixable.

The World. Around it. On a ship. Mostly.

Here's the miracle. It could have happened at any time on this rather photo-intensive trip when I would have had no opportunity to do a thing about it, or at any time in the past several years, during which I took thousands of pictures with that camera. And it happened the very moment the trip was OVER! Believe in Miracles. They happen.

Email Home:
N47° 35.007' W122° 20.766'
Seattle Container Port
Final update!
We're in the Container Port in Seattle, and I just have to finish packing, etc. then I'm off to the airport.
Hopefully all of the flights and connections will work as planned, and I'll be home late tonight - or, actually very early tomorrow morning. I've taken many pictures and have already started a slide show, so I'm sure I'll be inflicting it on you soon.
Thanks for all of your support and news from home while I've been away. I look forward to getting back to normal, seeing all of you, and hugging the grandbabies.
This will be the last time I use this account, so no need to reply to this or send anything to this address. I should have access to my regular email at this point,

The World. Around it. On a ship. Mostly.

and, hopefully, my phone will be operable.

The World. Around it. On a ship. Mostly.

Afterthoughts

26,000 miles. That's how far I traveled. More miles than if I had gone around the world at the Equator. North and South, I went from the Horn of Africa to the Bering Sea. And at the same time, I lived in a room and had as much freedom of movement as a prisoner in a penitentiary. Much more pleasant, of course, but I do remember an officer talking about the ship in terms of a prison.

Those of you who have thought throughout this that "if you haven't got anything nice to say, don't say anything at all," well – this book may be read by people who are on the verge of spending thousands of dollars to go on a freighter journey. Before spending that sort of dough, they ought to be told what they're likely to encounter. If I had read this before booking, I would still have gone, just done some things differently.

I found a quote from Mark Twain that sums up a lot of the "why" of this trip. It's from *"Some Rambling Notes of an Idle Excursion."* It goes: "….and then went wandering around here and there, in the solid comfort of being free and idle, and of putting distance between us and the mails and telegraphs." Couldn't have said it better myself, Mr. C., although I missed the "Mails and telegraphs" of the modern world. Perhaps they will figure a way to get full-fledged internet access onto such ships someday.

A lot of the time it's just your ship in its 30-mile-or-so-diameter bubble. It looks the same whether you're in the Atlantic, Indian or Pacific Ocean. Or the East China Sea. Or the Sea of Japan. The stars are different if you're in the Southern Hemisphere, but you'll be asleep. I napped 2-3 hours every day, at least while at sea. To quote one of the officers: "Sleep helps the time go." While

The World. Around it. On a ship. Mostly.

freighter travel may not at all times and in all ways be a great thing to do, it will turn out to be a great thing to have done. Make sure you've got a solitaire game on your laptop. If you don't know how to play, learn.

You may envision eating your meals with a convivial group of hearty, uniform-wearing, English-speaking seafarers at their table. And that could happen.

Or you could eat nearly every meal alone at your own table and if you see an officer in the mess, he'll be at another table, silent, probably alone (or speaking to a fellow-officer in a language you don't understand) wearing shorts and a t-shirt.

You may envision adventures ashore in exotic ports eating strange foods and buying silks and spices to take home. And that could happen.

Or you could arrive in every port at 1 AM, with an estimated time of departure of noon that same day, with a rule in place that everyone including passengers has to be back on board four hours before the ETD, with the result that, for nearly all of the time you'll be in those exotic ports, you'll be asleep.

On the trip toward Asia I'm sure we had many, or mostly, empty containers. Taking the empties back to be refilled with goods being imported. One piece of evidence for this would be the fact that they avoid the expense of the Suez Canal on the trip east. They aren't making as much money on the Asia-ward leg of the trip, so they don't want to pay the fees to use the canal. My line when asked "What was in the containers?" should be – "On the trip East, they contained American jobs being exported to Asia." But enough about politics.

So – bottom line – what do I think now that I've been back a while and no longer feel the ship as I walk on dry land? I value experiences. The ability to say "I have done that." I won't claim a

The World. Around it. On a ship. Mostly.

vast variety of such experiences, but those I have, I value beyond possessions. It's not even so much the memories. It's the fact, which can never be erased, that I have done it, whatever it is. I have sailed around the world on a ship. As Fred Astaire said – "They can't take that away from me."

My family was supportive of the idea, for which I thank them, and thank them as well for the emails they sent to me on the ship. They kept me grounded and helped fend off loneliness.

I can't claim to have forged any life-long friendships with the officers and crew, but I will remember them and value their friendliness and assistance on the trip. As I said, any complaints I may have made ("MAY have made? You complained through the whole book!") were due to the vicissitudes of freighter travel and of the agency I booked with, which shall continue to remain nameless, and not to any fault of the officers or crew or the shipping company who ran the ship.

If you are considering a trip on a container ship, go for it. But be very sure that you take nothing for granted, either as regards pre-trip arrangements, route, what you will find on the ship and what you will do as far as shore excursions. Keep an open mind and a sense of humor, and you'll be fine.